NLP for Leadership

Leverage NLP to Develop the Same Psychology and Skills as the Exceptional Leaders for Better Decision-making, a Clear Vision, More Courage and Self-leadership

By:

Jonatan Slane

Hello,

To fully master new NLP techniques, it´s best if you repeat them several times.

For your convenience we have assembled a PDF document with 34 most important NLP Techniques for you as a busy entrepreneur.

You can print these PDF or parts of these PDF as much as you want. You can place the NLP Technique where it´s the most convenient for you. This can be your bathroom mirror, the fridge in your kitchen or the monitor at your business. Whatever works for you.

If you want to be a productive entrepreneur:

Go to:
http://nlpforleadership.businessleadershipplatform.com/
or

Get the PDF with the 34 NLP techniques for Leadership

Print (parts of the) PDF

Start applying the NLP Techniques to **10x your business**

Now you´re ready to dive into the book.

Jonatan Slane

Business Leadership Platform

www.businessleadershipplatform.com

© Copyright 2019 - All rights reserved.

The content contained within this book may not be reproduced, duplicated or transmitted without direct written permission from the author or the publisher.

Under no circumstances will any blame or legal responsibility be held against the publisher, or author, for any damages, reparation, or monetary loss due to the information contained within this book, either directly or indirectly.

Legal Notice:

This book is copyright protected. It is only for personal use. You cannot amend, distribute, sell, use, quote or paraphrase any part, or the content within this book, without the consent of the author or publisher.

Disclaimer Notice:

Please note the information contained within this document is for educational and entertainment purposes only. All effort has been executed to present accurate, up to date, reliable, complete information. No warranties of any kind are declared or implied. Readers acknowledge that the author is not engaging in the rendering of legal, financial, medical or professional advice. The content within this book has been derived from various sources. Please consult a licensed professional before attempting any techniques outlined in this book.

By reading this document, the reader agrees that under no circumstances is the author responsible for any losses, direct or indirect, that are incurred as a result of the use of the information contained within this document, including, but not limited to, errors, omissions, or inaccuracies.

Table of Contents

Introduction   9
   Problem statement   9
   Solution   12
   Credible evidence   15
   The benefits of NLP   17

Chapter 1: NLP Explained   23
   Neuro-linguistic programming   23
   Practical techniques of NLP   29
   Internal maps of the world   37
   The history of NLP   39
   NLP in leadership   41
   The current status of NLP   44
   Applications of NLP Techniques   45

Chapter 2: Vision   49
   Benefits   50
   The SMART vision   56
   How to create a vision   59

Chapter 3: Thinking, problem-solving and decision making   65
   Thinking   66

Problem-solving	79
Decision making	90
NLP exercises for decision making	97

Chapter 4: Productivity and time management — 101

Personal productivity	101
Workplace productivity	107
Finding the state of flow	111
Time management	115

Chapter 5: Communication, negotiation, and presentation — 125

Communication	125
Presentation	148

Chapter 6: Anxiety and stress management — 153

Anxiety	153
Harnessing anxiety to excel	161
Stress	163

Chapter 7: Motivation — 169

NLP techniques to motivate yourself	169
NLP techniques to motivate others	179

Conclusion — 187

References — 193

Introduction

When you finally get a promotion into that new manager's office, you move in there with the excitement and expectations of a very fulfilled and decorated employee. However, once you settle in, you realize that you underestimated the challenges of being responsible for the productivity of not just yourself but everyone in your department as well. You are not alone in this though. Every leader charged with the supervision of a group of junior employees and delivering certain company goals will invariably find themselves facing a myriad of challenges in this quest. As you settle into your new office, you will have to adjust to a very different job description, fulfilling managerial rather than technical functions. And while you are at it, you can expect to face a whole new lineup of obstacles.

Problem statement

The following are some of the main problems new managers face in establishing their leadership.

- Not only do you have to work hard to be a better manager for your employer, but you also have to set an example for every other employee who looks up to you for guidance. You cannot do this with the same mentality you used to get there. Moreover, you will find that adapting to this demanding task can be very challenging. Not only must you ensure that the team works seamlessly, but you must also motivate every employee to work at his or her best to get there.

- Difficulty dealing with stress; a position comes with a corresponding amount of stress. The relationship between leadership and stress is directly proportional, which means that the more senior your position, the more stress you can expect to have to deal with. Managing your stress levels will turn out to be a critical aspect of your managerial career. At one point, you will just have to deal with the fact that popping Xanax does not really help you overcome your stress.

- Getting people on board with your vision; you are the kind of manager who creates a vision and mission statement for the department as soon as you take charge.

You have presented the ideal scenario to work towards, a plan you think makes absolute sense and one that you feel will motivate your team to achieve goals like they never did before. Except for one problem, you cannot get everyone to get on board with your vision. What do you do at times like these?

- Decision making is another problem that many managers face. In a stressful environment, with every decision you make carrying stakes so high they frighten you, it is a challenge to think clearly enough to make the decisions you need to make in the time you will be required to make them.

- As the manager, you are supposed to be the self-assured one. Everyone expects you to be the man or woman who makes tough choices and faces the consequences without blinking. So, what do you do when you feel your confidence slipping? Lack of confidence and self-esteem can be caused by many things: previous failures, problems in your personal life, deep-seated insecurities, and the fear of failure after setting huge goals for the department. Yet you are expected, as the leader of the group, to roll up your sleeves and lead the charge every single day. If you freeze up, the whole group freezes up and the momentum is lost.

- Communication skills are another area in which many managers struggle. Acquiring high competency in all forms of communication means that you can convince your team to believe in your vision and to apply their energies to the accomplishment of your goals. Decision making also requires the proper communication and deliberation of thoughts until you settle on the best one. Many managers have trouble communicating internally and with other people.

Solution

The solution to all these problems can be found in Neuro-Linguistic Programming (NLP). NLP is equivalent to learning the language of the mind. NLP is based on the premise that you can train your brain to adopt certain attitudes that will in turn empower you to achieve personal goals and objectives. Therefore, the things we say and the language we use to say to them work together with our thoughts to shape the reality in which we live.

This concept is referred to as the map of the world within NLP. More specifically, it refers to the perception of the world that you have created for yourself. Once you understand that you create your own perception of the world around you and that your perception of the world around you influences your reality, then you will be one step closer to arriving at the solution for all the problems stated above.

That is right; NLP is not something you get overnight. NLP is a process that starts with the recognition that you have more control over your own life and the things that happen around you than you previously thought and ends with actually gaining this control. In this book, we will get into the more minute details of NLP practices. We will also touch on the different ways that you can adopt NLP routines to improve your life in profound ways.

Albert Einstein famously said: "Everything is energy...match the frequency of what you want by your actions and you will automatically acquire it... it is pure physics." And it really is that simple. As soon as you have adopted the belief and action systems of the people who already have what you desire most, you will transform yourself into one of those people who have it and exhibit the habits you want to have by default.

By this logic, instead of transforming yourself into someone who is able to deal with stress, you simply transform into a person who deals perfectly with stress. The problem goes away completely and your transformation is almost effortless. It is the simple yet profound difference between "I'll believe it when I see it" and "If you believe it you will see it."

Credible evidence

Despite claims to the contrary, NLP has produced very tangible results in some of the most famous business, political, sports, and entertainment personalities. Because NLP challenges us to go out of our way to pursue excellence, the best leaders in the world are invariably the best examples of how using this strategy can bring success and immense personal development.

No single man better exemplifies this reality better than Sir Richard Branson, the founder of the Virgin Group of Companies. He has been quoted saying, "Dream big...set yourself impossible challenges...you will have to grow to catch up with them." This is perhaps the most succinct summarization of NLP. As stated above, it proposes that we can achieve the loftiest of goals if only we are willing to dare. Our brains can bridge the gap between our current abilities and our aims to grant us whatever we wish for.

In Sir Richard Branson's case, he started by overcoming dyslexia at a young age. Branson started Virgin Records, his first company, at the age of 20. He grew it rapidly and ultimately sold it for half a billion pounds just 20 years later. It was a painful decision that he had to make, but one that served him well, enabling him to start Virgin Galactic, the space travel company that is set to take the world by storm by offering commercial space travel. Here, he demonstrated a key quality of NLP by sacrificing something he valued for the chance to realize his goal. As much as you may want to use NLP to advance yourself, you must be ready and willing to pay the price.

Another instance where Richard Branson employed the concepts of neuro-linguistic programming was when he started Virgin Airways. He was stranded on his way to the Virgin Islands for a vacation with all flights canceled when he chartered a plane, solicited for customers among his fellow stranded travelers, and made it to his destination in time at no extra cost. This can-do mindset opened his eyes to the opportunities that existed in the travel business. He has since established numerous ventures in air, rail, and water transport, adding to his impressive pool of business holdings.

The benefits of NLP

Leaders who use NLP for self-development can attest to the numerous benefits it brings. These benefits include:

- Better decision making; NLP enables you to become more integrated with your thinking, which means that you are more likely to detect visual and kinesthetic (body language) tells in other people when taking in information. This heightened sensing ability increases your decision-making capabilities and makes you a better leader.

- Increased efficiency; the enhanced sensing and decision-making capabilities generated from neuro-linguistic programming empower you as a leader to streamline their work process. This means that when you use NLP, you are more likely to increase your own efficiency and that of your subordinates after some time.

- Higher productivity; increased decision making, and efficiency mean that you will be able to get more work done with fewer resources.

- Better communication skills; in essence, NLP is a way of thought that enhances communication for personal development. The first aspect of communication that receives a boost with NLP is internal. This empowers you to model the skills of the best leaders in your sector for your own success to manifest.

- Better vision; the first thing that you need to do on your journey to excellence using NLP is to clearly define your vision. This gives you the impetus to program your behavior in a way that makes it easier to achieve your personal goals. You cannot program your mind to succeed if you don't have a clear vision of where you want to go.

- Better influence and motivation skills; using NLP, you will learn to persuade your subordinates to act in a certain way. This means that you can influence their behavior in a way that supports your own goals. However, the skills you learn with NLP are altruistic, which means that your influence will be positive, and it will motivate the employees to work towards excellence for their own benefit as well as yours.

- Higher intrinsic motivation; NLP does not just motivate you to achieve your goals. It motivates you to become the person who is capable of achieving the goals you have set for yourself. It may seem inconsequential, but this intrinsic motivation means everything. With intrinsic motivation, you will be equipped with the tools to continue trying even in the face of failure—something a lot of people struggle with.

- Better stress management; the reason why the most successful leaders manage to push forward with their dreams despite facing failure is that they embrace failure as part of their success. In a similar way, NLP teaches you to embrace challenges in your quest for success. When you believe in yourself and you know that you will succeed despite the challenges you face, nothing can stress you out.

- Easier to disconnect and relax; NLP is therapeutic in nature. This means that you can disconnect from the stresses of life and unwind, recharging your mental energies for when you immerse yourself back into the rigors of pursuing success.

How do I know this? I have studied some of the best NLP practitioners of today for a long time—that's how. Tony Robbins uses NLP. He is one of the most successful business strategists and authors on Wall Street. Another prominent NLP practitioner is Eben Pegan. He is a multimillionaire who has taught numerous business leaders how to make money and sold hundreds of millions worth of products in practically every industry as a business leader himself. His specialty is using the principles of NLP to make products that connect with customers' feelings. Stefan James Pylarinos has adopted NLP to start a very successful career teaching other people to master their lives using NLP principles.

With such practical solutions available, why should you waste any more of your time and energy struggling to establish yourself as a leader? By learning a few simple NLP techniques, you can change both your life and your career dramatically. Not only will NLP improve your quality of life and ability to lead, but it will also empower you to enhance the lives of people around you for even greater productivity. In the words of Abraham Lincoln, the best time to prepare for the responsibilities of tomorrow is today. Give NLP a shot. I can promise that you will never live to regret it.

Chapter 1: NLP Explained

It is effective and it has been used by some of the most successful world leaders to attain massive success, but what exactly is NLP? In this chapter, we will cover the history and show you how leaders used the concepts attributed to NLP long before it was called NLP.

Neuro-linguistic programming

Neuro-linguistic programming is a style of using enhanced communication to nurture interactions with other people by combining the mind, the body, and our emotions. It is used to put us in a place where we can work smart and achieve more success. Another definition of NLP, one used by some of the greatest NLP practitioners, is "the study of excellence and the art of change." This is because NLP is concerned mostly with the enhancement of our own abilities to achieve success by studying and modeling our behavior after people who have already achieved success.

In practice, NLP combines the three scientific fields of neurology, linguistics, and programming. In neurology, the mind is the central processing unit of our brain. Everything that happens around us and to us is filtered into the conscious parts of our mind for us to experience through our minds. By understanding neural connections, you will be able to understand your own perception of the world and work to improve it for more success. The only way we can ever achieve success is by working towards it the right way. If your mind is not in the right position, you could spend years working towards success and never get there. Hindrances like self-doubt, fear of failure, and procrastination are the self-sabotaging tools that the unprepared mind uses to keep us from attaining victory.

The second aspect of NLP is, of course, language. Language encompasses everything from the way we think to the way we communicate our thoughts, both to ourselves and to others. More importantly, the linguistics part of NLP allows us to understand the language of the mind and overcome its weaknesses. Sometimes success is elusive because our minds are not aligned to the right position to acquire it. Understanding the language of the brain allows us to manipulate the brain using programming techniques. Therefore, the linguistic aspect of NLP bridges the gap between our minds and reality and empowers us to program ourselves into success.

NLP works only because we have the power to talk ourselves into succeeding. The way we do this is by brainwashing ourselves with the mindset of successful people. The programming aspect of NLP carries all the power of success. In essence, it teaches us that we can achieve any level of success as long as we can train our minds to think in a particular way. Want to succeed in business? Train your brain to think like a successful businessman. Want to lead your division to great new heights and improve your profile within the company? Train your brain to follow in the footsteps of a great business leader like Jack Welch. As long as you know the destination, you can teach your mind how to get you there.

By combining these three fields, we get neuro-linguistic programming. When you consider how hard it is to change behavior—if it were not so, we would not have such a thing as alcoholics or drug addicts—you can appreciate the power of NLP. It changes the way we think, addressing the reasons why we do the things we do to bring about change. This is the simplest definition of NLP; it is getting a user's manual for your own brain. This means that when you learn to use

NLP, you discover ways through which you can make your mind work in a certain way to generate a particular outcome.

NLP can also be defined as a system of tools and techniques that you manipulate to bring about your own success. With NLP, you learn to adopt the right attitude to achieve your goals. The techniques you adopt are aimed right at the subconscious mind, positioning it so that success comes almost automatically.

To sound less technical, NLP gives you a shortcut straight to your subconscious and allows you to place it in the right position to attract success into your life. This means that you condition your mind in such a way that, instead of sabotaging your efforts (which is very common when you have set lofty goals) it goes out of its way to foster your success. Your brain thus becomes the greatest asset in your pursuit of success.

Modeling

Within NLP, modeling is the process through which we adopt strategies, beliefs, language, and behavior from other people. We do this to model our own character to the successful people we look up to. For example, if you admire the work and life of Elon Musk, you can study and enumerate his behaviors, beliefs, and way of thinking.

If you model your behavior properly to a role model, you will find yourself systematically getting the same outcomes when you do something. Modeling allows you to automatically integrate a master's personality into your own. Because you engage in a critical analysis of a role model's behavior, you will often discover aspects of their personality that play a huge part in their success that even they are not aware of. You can then apply that aspect to your own work in a more pointed manner and attain massive success.

The process of modeling starts with suspending your own beliefs. This allows you to take up the mental models of the other person, starting with the psychology, beliefs, and strategies. After successfully integrating them into your own life, you will notice that your old beliefs, strategies, and psychology will start to manifest. You can never adopt another person's mental models without adding your own touch to them. This is the beauty of modeling. All you need to integrate a proven winning mentality into your life is to purposefully model your behavior to someone who has already succeeded.

Representation systems

The way we look at the world depends in a big way on the notions we hold of it. You could spend years living in a city and believing something about it based on the things that happen around you. But if you could move to a high point and view the entire city, your view of it would change dramatically.

For example, you could spend an eternity in a closed room that grows gradually stuffy, but because your senses adjust to the air within, you will not notice it until someone points it out or you walk out of the room and walk back. The same is true for a fresh room; you won't realize that a fruity-fresh room is fruity fresh until you experience different.

In the same way, we interpret information about events that happen around us based on previous experiences and the notions we have created about them. The processing of information takes place at the conscious and unconscious levels and impacts in a huge way on the way we do things.

With NLP, we focus on disrupting interpretations that were improperly formed but that nonetheless affect the way we do things.

Representation systems can also be great predictors of sensory preference, a useful tool for persuasion. For example, someone who communicates using visual descriptions like "see" would be better suited to visual presentations. The same goes for people who "feel"—appeal to their emotions—and those who "think" more—use logical language.

Practical techniques of NLP

Now let us get technical and look at the specific concepts that make up neuro-linguistic programming.

Anchoring

We are always making connections between the things we hear, see, and feel and events. For example, if you set a particular song as your alarm and it is the first thing you hear once you wake up, your brain will make an association with it. This connection is even stronger when you are in an emotional state. This is because a connection is made between the specific stimulus and a very specific feeling.

In NLP, these associations are called anchors. They are created using touch, sight, and sound.

More importantly, NLP teaches us how to deliberately trigger a certain emotion using these anchors. For example, listening to your alarm song in the middle of the day will most probably make you anxious and alert.

To successfully create anchors from the things we encounter, you must detect the emotions associated with every stimulus of touch, sound, and sight. That is why your workspace should be personalized. From a picture of your family, pet, or your graduation, we all need something to remind us why we give our work everything we've got. Your anchor will help you to find and keep your focus on the most important thing.

Future pacing

Future pacing is used in two ways. First and foremost, future pacing is used to gauge the effectiveness of an NLP intervention. If after an intervention someone reacts to a future prospect the same way they reacted to it before getting it, then the intervention hasn't been successful. An intervention is said to have been successful when the person reacts as desired to triggers.

In the second application of future pacing, "what-if" scenarios are painted with the intention of embedding change into the psyche.

To a large extent, the mind is incapable of telling apart visualized and real events, which means that reactions are usually the same whether stimuli are real or simulated.

Visualization is one of the most important techniques in NLP. In particular, positive visualization plays a big part in motivating people to action. Sometimes, visualizing something you find hard to do as having already happened can help you in actually getting it done. This is especially true for those situations when you find yourself procrastinating.

And when making a choice between two things, visualizing each one of them as the reality and gauging your reaction to it can help you to figure out the best choice.

Swish

Every thought comes with an attached emotion, just like every memory does. The swish pattern is a model of thought that advocates swapping the emotions associated with a bad thought with the one you have regarding a good memory. The swish technique works because our minds are easily deceived and can be made to feel a certain way with the right stimuli, genuine or simulated.

More importantly, what this means is that you have it within your power to change how you feel about that scary interview from anxious and terrified to confident and self-assured. All you need to do is bring to mind a previous experience when you felt good and swap the memory picture of the event with the one that comes to mind when you think about the thing that terrifies you. When at last the event does transpire, you will find yourself looking forward to it and actually being confident and self-assured.

Reframing

Every event takes on a very different meaning when looked at using a different frame. For example, a horrible event that you can't see a way out of right now might be funny when considered in the long term. Reframing occurs in a few distinct ways:

Context; this entails looking at a bad situation and finding a positive spin to focus on instead. Failed the midterm? At least there's the final exam to make up for it. Failed the final exam too? Well, it is an average of annual performance that matters. Does annual performance suck? At least you're still alive...See, anything can be spun positively when the context is adjusted.

Content; NLP presumes that everything people do is motivated by positive intentions. If you want to live positively, finding and nurturing that good intention in everyone can be very important.

Well-formed outcome

Instead of setting a goal that you will reach and settle on, NLP suggests creating a well-formed outcome that will force you to continue working at something even after getting there. This is the standard way of setting goals in NLP. To do this, we break down the goal into smaller parts. For example, a goal like "I want my business to outdo the rest of the industry this year" breaks down into smaller objectives like "I want to win over more customers from my competitors" and "I want to be more efficient than my competitors." These goals will push you to keep working because they are a work in progress.

Ecology

The ecology technique teaches that you must look at the consequences that the pursuit and attainment of the well-formed outcome will have on your life from every angle. This enables you to prepare for the changes that will come and sacrifices you will have to make to accommodate them.

Parts integration

The parts integration technique seeks to harmonize the different pieces of ourselves that are usually in conflict arising from the different beliefs and perceptions that we hold. Integrating all parts of our psyche allows us to quell the internal conflict that often hinders our ability to achieve the goals we set for ourselves.

VKD

VKD is an abbreviation for Visual Kinesthetic Dissociation. VKD is aimed at eliminating bad feelings we have about past events. A common strategy of VKD therapy is to replay a traumatic event over and over again in a dissociated state until we no longer react badly to it. Visual triggers like pictures and film are used to trigger the bad feelings and then positive reinforcement is used to enable one to overcome them.

Metaphor

NLP trainers use metaphors to connect with the unconscious mind of their clients. Metaphors are given in three different types: shallow, deep, and embedded. While shallow metaphors are simple, comprised of comparisons or similes, deep metaphors have multilayered meanings that give the trainer deeper access to the client's source code for behaviors.

Embedded metaphors, on the other hand, contains a number of metaphors that have been linked together. Stories have given in an embedded metaphor often don't make sense, which means that the trainer is in a better position to manipulate the client's subconscious mind for improved learning and healing.

Metaphors create mind shifts because they imply relationships and force the client to fill in the blanks. This allows for new interpretations and insights.

State management

The emotional states we find ourselves in at a particular time have a huge impact on the ability we have to do things. When you are emotionally balanced, you will be more likely to focus on the job than when your mind is in chaos. As such, it is important that we maintain the state that is most conducive to the attainment of a goal. This entails managing relationships, setting a schedule, and reinforcing positive behavior.

Covert hypnosis

Any time you do something unconsciously, you are essentially in a trance. This includes automatic body functions like breathing, blinking, etc. At other times, we do things without being actively involved. Like when you drive home but don't really pay attention to the road because you have made the trip thousands of times or tuning a boring colleague out when he or she prattles on. The unconscious mind takes over in these situations, putting us in a state of semi-hypnosis.

Covert hypnosis in management is mainly used to satisfy the embedded desires of employees by making the job have a deep personal meaning. This way, the worker finds their job deeply satisfying and meaningful and you as the manager get better results from your committed workers. Any time unconscious emotions are appealed to, people react positively. It is hypnotic in that you get them to do what you want, and it is covert in that they actually do want to do what you want them to do. However, you must be careful with this particular technique. There will always be the accompanying temptation to misuse it for selfish ends.

Internal maps of the world

We touched lightly on the internal maps of the world in the introduction. In this section, we shall delve into the topic in more detail. How exactly does your internal map of the world affect your success?

The internal map of the world is what forms when the mind/body blends together with the things we say, or language. This is something that will always happen eventually as long as we are actively interpreting the world around us and forming some understanding of it. Therefore, the view we hold of the world often plays the greatest part in determining how we act, the things we believe are possible, and the goals we set.

The internal map of the world is the expression of not just our current perception of what the world around us looks like but also the perception we have of the future and possibilities for success. As such, just like in the real world, your internal map of the world determines the jurisdiction you perceive yourself as having. If you think you have a very limited role to play in attaining success in your career or any other aspect of your life, then your internal map of the world is probably tiny and limiting. You cannot see how you would be able to push the borders and come into a greater state of being: owning more, achieving more, and being more.

Your map of the world determines how you feel about yourself and the world. It also plays a part in your day-to-day actions. If your current map is impoverished, you will experience insurmountable problems in your quest for success. If your mental map is abundant, your life will reflect this.

The good thing about the map of the world is that you can change it. With NLP, you can shift your perception of the world from impoverished and limited to abundant and unlimited. You can get the motivation to wage war on limitations and expand your borders outwards. Because only you have the power to mark the territory you occupy, you can redraw the map to make it as big as you want.

A limited view of the map of the world is that it is the way we perceive the world. Looking at it broadly, however, you can draw endless meanings from it. Adding to the idea that you create your own map according to your own personal desires, we can add that your stability and ability to maintain the highest ideals or state of being depends, like in a real-life country, on the neighboring countries. The people you surround yourself with can either empower you to achieve more (expand your borders) or hinder you from succeeding (infringe on your territory).

To change a destructive internal map of the world, you need only modify or change patterns of belief and behavior with useful ones. But first, you must change the internal representation of your map of the world to increase behavioral flexibility.

The history of NLP

NLP was created by John Grinder and Richard Bandler in the early 1970s. The two authors built their concept on the model of self-realization created by Abraham Maslow in the 1940s and modeled it around the work of world-famous psychotherapists of the time. Initially, the aim of their model was to determine what made their admired therapists special and how they could transfer this specialness to other people.

From the time Grinder and Bandler formed it, NLP has gone through a few transformations. Prominent among them are NLPure, NLPt, NLPeace, and NLPsych.

NLPure

NLPure is the original NLP that was started by John Grinder and Richard Bandler. Its main focus was success and enthusiasm. The founders were joined in advocating success and enthusiasm through neuro-linguistic programming by numerous other scholars. This paved the way for the growth of NLP, with speakers teaching enormous groups of people the benefits of NLP through seminars.

NLPt

In the 80s, health and the joy of living gained more appreciation among proponents of NLP at the same time that applications in psychotherapy spread. The widespread acceptance of NLPt led to the creation of associations like the European Association of Neuro-Linguistic Psychotherapy (EANLPt).

NLPeace

At the turn of the century, people started to apply NLP to spirituality and created the third wave of NLP. More and more people were now seeking to use NLP to improve their meaning of life. Applications for general improvement also went up at around this time.

NLPsych

NLPsych is the most recent improvement in NLP. Suggested after a 2006 study of the application of NLP, it substitutes programming with psychology and requires NLP practitioners to be trained in psychology. More than any other version of NLP, NLPsych relies on scientific methods. The increased reliance on scientific methods also helps to change the narrative that NLP is a pseudoscience, a claim that has dogged it since its inception.

NLP in leadership

NLP was practiced by some of the most popular world leaders long before it was even invented. To prove this point, we will discuss the five universal qualities of a good leader and demonstrate how they fall in line with the concepts of neuro-linguistic programming.

Self-restraint

Leaders are often faced with extremely stressful situations. The best trial of the mettle of a leader is their temperament in times of crisis. NLP holds the idea that with self-reflection, we can work past emotional triggers of anger and develop a more withstanding type of patience that will help us weather any adversity that comes in life. A leader like Harry Truman, who led the world calmly through the cold war, is a textbook study on NLP leadership concepts.

Leading by example

Pretty much any successful leader has led by inspiring their followers to do something they would normally balk at doing, simply because the leader himself was willing to lead by example. Vision- setting and selling your vision to your followers is one of the most important facets of NLP training.

Learning from mistakes

Leaders are not made when things are going well; they are made when everything is going horribly wrong. It is also believed that you are not a leader until you have failed because failure is the biggest, most challenging test any leader faces. Notably, every prominent leader from Nelson Mandela to Franklin Roosevelt to Richard Branson and Albert Einstein—both of whom overcame dyslexia and went on to achieve great success in their respective fields—proves that challenges make a good leader.

NLP teaches us to be bold while taking calculated risks. Mistakes are a part of life and we need not worry about making them. Rather, we should learn from them. Leaders were doing this even before Richard Bandler and John Grinder conceptualized their NLP model.

Proper communication

Leaders use communication tools to cultivate loyalty and motivate action from their followers. NLP also teaches us to develop our self-awareness tools and enforce positive behavior from employees.

Emotional intelligence

NLP is essentially a study in emotional intelligence. We learn to identify our own emotions and the emotions of our subordinates as well as how we can capitalize on both for more productivity. The world's most successful leaders display a common quality of extremely high emotional intelligence. They are able to detect the emotions of their followers and position themselves in such a way that they harness them for the greater good.

The current status of NLP

Today, NLP is taught by hundreds of thousands of coaches and thousands of books have been written about it over time. The people who use NLP are able to replicate the success of other, more successful people to achieve success in their own lives. The main reason why people are drawn to NLP is that it works in such profound ways. Coincidentally, it is for the same reason that many people doubt its effectiveness, even without first having tried it out.

Even with maestros like Tony Robbins (who learned NLP directly from Grinder) screaming the benefits of NLP from the biggest stages in the world, the opposition to NLP remains. In the meantime, the people who practice it succeed and even many of those who don't consciously practice it will match the strategies taught by NLP coaches. One of the reasons why NLP faces so much opposition is that it has been commercialized to a greater extent than other psychological models of the 20th century. In spite of the opposition, studies have increasingly shown that people who use NLP find success a lot more frequently than any other group.

All in all, NLP practitioners have created exceptionally powerful tools for the improvement of communication and neural processes over the years that are still paying off to date. Applications include in the fields of psychotherapy, education, leadership, counseling, and creativity. And even though the scientific proof for NLP is still lacking, the relationship between mind, communication, and reality are widely accepted.

Applications of NLP Techniques

Neuro-linguistic programming has numerous applications. This is because NLP techniques are incredibly powerful tools when applied to real-life situations. They are capable of empowering profound change. However, the power of NLP is directly proportional to the ardor of the person applying them. In this section, we look at some common NLP applications.

Personal development

NLP is essentially a self-development tool. Through NLP, we learn to reflect on our own actions, build confidence, and communicate effectively. More importantly, NLP teaches us the surest way we can go about achieving personal goals—modeling our behavior after that of someone more successful. This is a surefire way of attaining your potential and the reason why men like Tony Robbins have achieved the success they have achieved to date.

From the actions of business leaders like Richard Branson, Elon Musk, and many more, we also learn the concepts of aiming for the sky even when our current skills do not match up. Using the concepts of NLP, as long as you want it badly enough, your mind can always find a way to get you there.

Achieve goals

Neuro-linguistic programming has also been applied in the workplace to empower leaders to achieve work-related goals. By applying the concepts used by the most successful of business leaders at the workplace, you will meet and exceed workplace goals, increase the productivity of your department, and guarantee your progression up the corporate ladder.

Therapy

NLP has also been used in the treatment of psychological disorders. For example, people with anxiety, depression, and low confidence (low self-esteem issues) can apply NLP to find relief.

In the rest of this book, we will focus on the ways through which you can use NLP in your workplace to improve your management skills. This is an important subject of discussion seeing as you will be expected to provide leadership for subordinates, have a vision for the group, and figure out a way to get there. And unlike senior management positions in a company, lower-level managers are judged more by the results of their own work, i.e., the results posted in their division or department. If something happens that prevents you and your team from achieving your goal, the responsibility lies with you and you only.

So, read on to discover how you can apply the techniques of NLP discussed in this chapter to different aspects of your job as a manager. These include vision setting, decision making and problem-solving, time management, communication and negotiation, stress management, and motivation.

Chapter 2: Vision

A clear vision and mission statement is indispensable when you are leading a group of people. It is what creates a strong foundation for you as you tackle the difficulties that come along the way to success. When your career is guided by a clear-cut vision, you will always have something to consult when making those difficult decisions and answering unexpected questions. It also means that you will be less likely to fall for distractions that come along the way. In this chapter, we will talk about vision setting and pursuing with NLP.

The most effective NLP technique for setting and selling your vision is future pacing. It has been used by legendary leaders, especially in the political field, to great effect. In the current age, few leaders stand out as having sold their vision to the public more than Martin Luther King, Junior. His "I have a dream" speech electrified a nation to action and ultimately brought civil rights to millions of Americans.

But arguably more effective in employing future pacing was the forty-fourth President of the United States, Barack Obama. In his 2004

Democratic Convention speech, the hitherto unheard-of senator from the tiny state of Hawaii rose to overnight eminence by leading the American public to visualize a rosy future with his "Yes We Can" speech. Four years later, he moved into the most prestigious office in the world— the White House. All this because he had a vision and was able to make others believe in it.

The reason why a vision holds such great sway over people's emotions is that there is the perception that it is the only part of the time that we can affect today. The past is already gone, and the present is the product of what we did in the past. Only the future remains open for exploration. If you can manage to create the best idea of a future, selling it to your employees will be easy enough as long as you take their needs and desires into account.

Benefits

And on a personal level, you can expect to witness the following benefits.

Improved self-confidence

As we mentioned above, a vision statement takes into account everything you want to achieve and compresses it in a way that is easy to reference. When creating a vision, you first determine the ideal destination you would like to get to. You think one year, two years, five years, or more into the future and define the goals you would like to have already achieved. The goals allow you to focus your energies on the things that will propel you towards your ideal future. With focused energy comes increased efficiency and with it, more results and confidence in your own abilities.

Moreover, as you deliberate on your future for the purpose of goal setting, you will notice that it is easy to indulge your more ambitious tendencies. After all, it is in the future and everything is possible. But once you set the goals and break them down to the present where a simple task is what sets you on the path to the main vision, you will realize that it is very possible to attain the lofty goal you set. You sure will get a bump of self-confidence then.

A leader is only as good as the people he leads allows him or her to be. A common goal is one of the most rejuvenating incentives in the workplace, but it is also true that people are more motivated when the goal they pursue as a team is even bigger. So, when your employees believe in your vision, they will work even harder to bring about its actualization. The dedication of your employees (and the success it will undoubtedly bring about) will leave you feeling more confident and self-assured than you have felt in ages.

Reduces stress

Leadership is a very stressful career. The responsibilities are greater, accountability is to a higher authority, and you will be granted very limited room for mistakes. You will definitely feel the pressure of your new position more. Managing the pressure can get especially stressful. If you are not careful, the stress could get to you and drastically affect your ability to deliver. This is where a vision and the ability to visualize the future come in handy.

First off, a vision reduces your stress levels by giving you something to focus on. The goal becomes your worth to the senior managers, your employees, and the customers. If it is a good enough goal, your singular dedication to its attainment will leave you feeling empowered and driven. Even when failure crosses your path, you can shrug it off and carry on.

Now, when pursuing a vision with NLP strategies, you have another advantage that other people do not have. You can visualize the future. Visualization is a powerful motivation tool that will transport you to a magical world of blissful achievement in your most stressful situations, remind you why you are doing what you are doing, and leave you feeling more positive than ever. Moreover, when you can visualize yourself having already achieved something, your belief in your ability to attain it increases and you feel less pressure to be perfect.

Improves thinking and decision making

Roughly 80% of what you will be doing in your new job will involve thinking. You will get a lot of questions for which you cannot produce a direct answer each and every day. You will be called in to solve huge problems and be asked to make a choice between two impossible situations so often you will not believe it. This is a lot of mental activity. If you are not careful, it could easily overwhelm you.

But when you come up with a defined vision, your thinking will be compartmentalized based on its contribution to the ultimate realization of your goals. Every question posed, every decision and every problem will be answered the same way—using the checklist of your vision. The more you prioritize the vision in your work, the more passionate you will become about it. More passion increases your chances of actually accomplishing what you set out to accomplish in your vision.

In 1990, Microsoft was facing a dilemma in regard to its strategic relationship with leading computer manufacturer IBM. Started ten years prior, the relationship had been vital in the quest of Microsoft to become the best software company in the world. Behind this vision was a young man named Bill Gates. He had navigated the murky waters of software publishing from the onset and proven himself to be a ferocious leader. The vision of a world-dominating Microsoft had originated with Gates. His partner Paul Allen was more content making software than conquering the world.

Cutting ties with IBM was a decision unlike any other Gates, or few other men, had ever made. It would be akin to jumping off a ship with nothing more than a sailboat in the middle of the ocean.

Will the fuel last you to shore? Will you be able to navigate? Is it even a good idea?? Well, for Bill Gates, the way to answer that question was simplified by his NLP-like thinking. He had a great vision, one that IBM was, as of 1990, frustrating. As much as the decision looked like a terrible idea at the time, he made it without flinching. And his company emerged even stronger from the ordeal.

Removes complexity

Have you ever been so worried about a seemingly huge problem, only to find the decision about how to solve it really easy? You see, this is a common trick our brain uses when it is anxious—it magnifies a small problem. Evolutionarily speaking, this means that we take seriously things like cold weather and avoid coming down with a cold. On the job, you will find yourself feeling better about firing an underperforming employee if you consider that it will free him or her up to find a better place of work and enable you to hire a better-suited employee. When you look at the bigger picture, you go back to the core foundation and consider them more wholesomely. The result, you will find, is that the answer always becomes clearer.

As I said, the best visions can usually be summarized using simple phrases. This condensation removes the complexity and ambiguity and points you in the right direction. Whether you are answering questions, making decisions, or solving complex problems, you can arrive at a solution faster when you get down to the basics. Ask pointed questions. Find out the crux of the matter. Have a clear idea of what is in question and then you can endeavor to find a solution. And as usual, the only viable solution is one that helps you to realize your vision.

The SMART vision

Future pacing using NLP follows a very simple and very universal tactic- the SMART approach. Specific goals are easier to make but surprisingly hard to implement. Think of a vague goal such as, "Be the best department in the company." Unless your company holds an annual gala where it awards the best department in the company, this is too subjective a goal. You can claim to be the best because you have a margarita machine in the office on Friday, but that is neither here nor there. Specific goals are also measurable. For example, growth in sales volumes quarter to quarter, profit levels, and

ROI. These are quantifiable units that you can objectively track.

It is very tempting to set goals that are so wildly out of reach that they become untenable. This will derail your vision. Achievable goals are easier to reach because it is within our power to attain them. I am not saying that you should not aim high. Just know your limitations and keep your goals within them. This is also why the next quality of a SMART goal is realistic. The attainment of the goal must not be so out of the ordinary that it requires a miracle. It is much better to shoot within your capabilities and actually win than to aim for the improbable and lose.

Finally, a smart vision should be timed. Using NLP, setting a timeline for goals follows a very specific process. It entails thinking about something that will happen in a few hours' time, tomorrow, next week, next month, in the next year, the next two years, and so on and so forth. The things you think about will usually come from the same direction. Moreover, you will realize that the ideas generated by your mind are either spontaneous or there is a tug-of-war before you settle on an idea.

Within that tug-of-war is the ideal goal to aim for and another, either higher or lower, that your biased mind is trying to push through. If you are more ambitious, the alternative will be far above what your subconscious knows is attainable. Through focused timeline thinking, you can uncover from the deepest parts of your brain the limits of your abilities and strive to set goals by them.

How to create a vision

Martin Luther King, Jr., and Barack Obama shared their visions with the American public to great rewards. Analyzing these two visionary leaders, one tactic stands out far above the rest. Their visions are best summarized in a few words. "Yes we can" and "I have a dream" are both slogans that represented a broader vision, but with time they came to be the vision. When selling your own vision, you should keep in mind that humans are associative in nature. If you can compress your vision into a few words, your followers will subscribe more wholeheartedly to the core ideals.

Okay, so a vision is clearly very important. It creates clarity where confusion hitherto existed and plots a clear path to the future. But how exactly do you come up with one? And how do you put it into action? In this section, we will look at the most effective NLP exercises to practice and execute in relation to future pacing and setting a vision for you and your department.

Discover

Creating a vision is all about plotting a path to the attainment of your goals. On a personal level, you simply reach into your heart and find your purpose in life, then come up with a way to get there. As a leader, you will be responsible for the attainment of the dreams of all your employees, the company, and your customers. You must be very clear about what you are aiming for. This is why the first process is discovery. In discovery, you ask yourself a few questions:

- What are the most valuable things to (1) the customer, (2) my subordinates, and (3) my bosses?

If you can find the answer to this question, you will have in your hands the tools you need to reconcile the different demands of your job into a single aim. By visualizing, you can brainstorm ways through which you will manage to satisfy everyone who relies on you for leadership.

- What is your resource endowment?

Your ability to do anything is always restricted by the resources you have to accomplish it. This goes for time, money, and more importantly, goodwill. Whatever vision you come up with will govern your actions into the foreseeable future, so you must be really sure before you embark on the journey.

Find your heroes

NLP owes a big part of its power to motivate people to succeed in the techniques of modeling. While creating a vision, you must take advantage of modeling and find inspirational figures who have been at your position and worked their way to so much greater success. These role models become your heroes and heroines and you model your vision—at least in part—to their behavior.

There are not many celebrity business leaders who rose to prominence through employment, but the few outstanding ones left a mark in their companies and entire industries. Lee Iacocca is one such leader. He employed NLP concepts like rapport building and future pacing to lead two of the world's biggest automotive companies. At Ford, he rose up the ranks from a lowly sales manager to CEO. At Chrysler, he rescued an American icon from bankruptcy. The outstanding quality of Iacocca's management career is that he always had a vision. Some of the most successful cars at Ford, like the Mustang, were developed under his leadership. And at

Chrysler, he orchestrated the acquisition of the American Motor Corporation simply to bequeath the highly profitable Jeep model to the company.

Dream

After discovering the thing your dependents value most and the resources you have to achieve them, you have to commit to a particular course of action. Using NLP, the ideal way to set a dream is by closing your eyes and transporting yourself into the future. Here, keeping the facts you acquired in discovery, you envision a world where you have already achieved them.

Immersion helps you to discover specific details about your vision that will enable you to tackle future questions and problems with conviction. This step of the vision setting is akin to meditation, whereby you follow the initial train of thought (the dream) and then let it transport you to a make-believe world where your vision has come to life. You will obviously be biased, thinking about the common complaints you get at work, problems you encounter, and challenges that face you. But here is the key; as you envision a world in which these problems are nonexistent or you have prevailed over them, your mind will become enlightened to find ways of solving them so that your goals are indeed achieved.

Conscious dreaming can either be guided using covert hypnotism or you could do it alone. Either way, it helps your mind conceive a world of success which motivates you to work towards it. And with a team, you can do this even more effectively because you will call every employee to share their dreams, right down to the specific ways they think you can attain them as a team. The advantage here is that an employee working in IT is in a better position to imagine the future of IT, and the same with accounts, sales, and every other division.

Design

As you dream up a new world where you are achieving your goals, focus on the most important things. You must work towards the most compelling vision, not the easiest one. It is very important that you make the vision achievable because unrealistic dreams are very often unachievable. In fact, an unreal objective is one of the leading causes of procrastination.

And having figured out a compelling vision, the next thing is to find out what you need to do to achieve it. This means you research and educate yourself on the process of achieving whatever it is that you want to be. Along with the skills you must learn to be in a position to achieve the dream, find other people who can lend a hand.

When designing a vision for your department, selling your employees and employers on the idea is imperative. The employees will play a huge part in the actualization of the vision and your employer will provide you with the resources and the goodwill to pursue it. The worst mistake you can make at this point is to think that you can do it all by yourself. Teamwork is the key.

Destiny

The last process of crafting a vision is defining it in a succinct and direct manner. Here, you write down all the vision and mission statements that make up your dream. You must be sure to write the vision statement in a positive and affirmative tone. It should also be provocative enough that everyone involved in the quest to achieve it will be motivated to work.

After reading through it to make sure that it is what you want, apply yourself to the vision and don't give in until you realize it.

Chapter 3: Thinking, problem-solving and decision making

I have said this before and I will say it again. The most important job description of a manager is thinking. Improving your ability to think, problem-solve, and make decisions can be a huge boost to your career. On the thinking front, the most crucial advantage of clarity empowers you to spot opportunities. Superior decision-making capabilities mean that you can do what you need to do to take advantage of the opportunities.

Problem-solving is another important skill for managers. It comes in handy when you are facing a crisis at work, improving service delivery, or arbitrating disagreements between your subordinates, among other applications. In this chapter, we will look at different ways to use NLP to improve your thinking, problem-solving, and decision-making skills.

Thinking

To become a good business leader, you must be capable of higher-order thinking. Only in the military and disciplined forces can you possibly scrape through without being equipped with the best thinking capabilities. But even military leaders have to be good tacticians, and creating good tactics requires that you have a good brain on your shoulders and the ability to use it.

There are two main styles of thinking: creative and critical. A good leader combines elements of both to come up with unique, well-thought-out solutions to business problems. If you want to become a good leader, then you must start by fixing the way you think. You must be aware of the mental models that are responsible for your actions, understand the conscious and unconscious mind and how the two affect your life, know the right questions to ask, understand associations, and recognize the shortcomings that exist in your thought process.

Mental Models

Mental models are the ways we analyze and understand the world. Mental models are often based on basic principles that we use to simplify complex events that happen all around us. Mental models are often limited and stereotypical, but we can adjust them by objectively analyzing new information rather than relying on our old stereotypes. And because mental models inform every single decision we make, we should be careful to moderate the sort of thinking that governs our thinking. In this section, we will look at some of the mental models that hinder our progress as leaders.

For example, if you micromanage your employees, this is because you have a jack-of-all-trades mental model. You only trust in yourself to get things done, which could turn out to be a huge burden. Even if there is evidence to support your assumption that you get things done more effectively than your subordinates, continuing down micromanagement lane will lead you to overwork, burnout, and mess-ups. Delegating is an even greater mark of a good leader because it means you have put together a team you can trust. It also frees your mind up to think about the more important things like the long-term strategy of your division.

Another destructive mental model that you may be laboring under is perfectionism. As much as you must always strive for excellence, chasing perfection will leave you exhausted and anxious.

What's more, you will probably never get to the point of utmost satisfaction with your achievements, which is crucial for motivation and inspiration.

Snap decision making is a mental model that very often comes disguised as an aptitude. People who do it often believe that it is a strength to exploit and be proud of. But it is anything but and could, in fact, be derailing your career advancement. When you make snap decisions, you fail to take the time to consider the consequences of doing something. This could have disastrous implications not just for you but for the company and your employees. Snap decision making also means that you expose yourself to subliminal and deliberate manipulation.

To make it from a regular employee to manager takes a lot of hard work and hours of routine work. The more you get done, the greater the rewards you reap. This tends to program our minds in a certain way, leaving most of our minds modeled to believe that productivity can only be achieved by working long and grueling hours. This could not be further from the truth as a leader. Your job in this new capacity is to govern, which includes organizing your team based on the competency of each member. If you have created the mental model of working late into the night, neglecting your work-life balance, and sleeping a few hours every night, you must realize that this simply won't cut it. Leadership is a whole new ballgame and you must upgrade your skills to make it.

The other mental model most business leaders create for themselves is the superman complex. Managers with this mental model live under the assumption that they don't need anyone to help them perform their duties. While admirable, you must learn to tame the inclination to take the blame for everything that goes wrong (or right) in your department.

Instead of using these negative mental models, you should instead copy the thinking style of leaders like Ray Dalio, a man who has used second-order thinking perfectly to establish a very successful career in stock market investing. Thinking about consequences to the second, third, and fourth-order means that nothing will ever find you unawares and that you will always be a few steps ahead.

The conscious and unconscious mind

What is stopping you from adapting to your new role as a manager? Most people will answer this question by citing external causes that are completely out of their direct control. This is the wrong approach. For a better understanding of how you can use your mind to understand and influence your internal world, you will have to use NLP. With NLP, our mind influences our thinking on two levels: the conscious and the unconscious.

Conscious thought is done deliberately. The concept is simple; for a positive impact on your inner thoughts, you will have to think positively. It is quite effective and is widely used around the world to affect constructive actions.

However, the conscious mind is limited by its capacity to retain information. At best, we are able to follow nine simultaneous bits of information. Just think about it. Do you even memorize your phone number (or any phone number) ten digits at a time? No, you do it three or four digits at a time because this information is far easier to collect, store, and recall. Sleight-of-hand magicians and other tricksters also use their knowledge of the limitations of the conscious mind to trick their audiences.

As a manager, your diary will be filled with important meetings, interviews, and business functions. Your chances of excelling at these activities depend on your ability to absorb and retain massive amounts of data and keep it at your fingertips, the agenda for a staff meeting, for example, including the exact agenda that carries an important issue you intend to raise. All this information will be stored in your conscious mind.

The unconscious mind, on the other hand, is the store of information that we don't need at this exact moment. In addition to the nine bits of information you hold at the fore of your mind, there is a whole lot of information that you are not consciously aware of. If you can manage to unlock this part of your mind, you will unlock a massive bank of information, some of which you wouldn't even be aware of holding. In one study, anesthetized patients remembered word for word the conversations that went on around them while they were being operated on.

Even though you will hardly ever be aware of it, your unconscious controls every aspect of your life. It also responds to all external stimuli without any prompting whatsoever. So, even if your conscious mind sees success in a straightforward situation but your unconscious mind is prompted by some random stimuli to go negative, you will somehow wind up sabotaging yourself.

NLP intervenes in this kind of a situation to create congruence. Congruence means that you have aligned your brain and your actions with positive thoughts and commit totally to the achievement of the desired outcome. In the event that you are finding it hard to focus on positive thoughts, you can recall the positive events of your past and use them to motivate yourself when negativity interferes with current actions. With 10 billion neurons in our brains, the possible connections we can make in our minds are infinite. Only when we don't utilize the brain to the maximum do we limit ourselves in life.

NLP Exercise—Circles of excellence

To create a resourceful state of mind and body any time you need it, perform the following time-proven exercise.

1. Stand at a point with six feet of space ahead of it.

2. In your mind, draw a circle on this floor. Make the circle as visually attractive as you'd like.

3. Think of an encouraging phrase like "Yes I Can," "I Can Do It," or "I Am Success" that motivates you.

4. Think of one time when you exceeded your highest expectations and go back to that time. Try to recall it as vividly as possible, including the smells, tastes, or colors associated with the memory.

5. Let this memory fill you up, then say your phrase out loud, take a deep breath, and step inside the circle.

6. Inside the circle, give yourself up to the memory, taking the time to enjoy the sensation of excelling.

7. Now think about the situation you are about to face and see yourself excelling beyond your wildest dream. Let the confidence of your past victory fill you up.

You are set to go and conquer the world!

Logical fallacies

Few things hamper success more than shortcomings in thinking. In logical fallacies, false ideas created from flawed opinions and personal biases get in the way of sound thinking. It is very important to learn how to argue or reason without resorting to unsound arguments and also to have the ability to spot fallacies in other people's opinions. Let's look at logical fallacies in short, shall we?

You see, there are several types of them, and all differ from each other in various ways. First off, there are formal and informal fallacies. Formal fallacies are also called deductive because they entail a clear-cut error in inferring a conclusion from a reasonable argument. A reasonable argument contains a premise, evidence, and a conclusion. For example:

All scientists are curious

Bill is a scientist.

Therefore, Bill must be curious.

Let us look at the argument above from a different angle.

All scientists are curious.

Bill is curious

Therefore, Bill must be a scientist.

This constitutes a deductive fallacy based on the fact that we used the evidence of being (curiosity) rather than the state of being (a scientist) to make our conclusion.

Informal fallacies are inductive in nature. They support the conclusion but they are not necessarily completely true. You can only be sure of the accuracy of a conclusion to a limited level of certainty. For example, the following argument would have been correct in 1958 but incorrect in 1959.

The coast of Alaska has never been hit by a tornado.

Therefore, the coast of Alaska will not be hit by a tornado this year.

Errors in reasoning can either be logical or factual. If you take a valid argument and make the wrong conclusion based on the wrong evidence presented, you will technically be right (logically) but wrong because you can't make a valid conclusion from the wrong information.

Using metaphors in NLP, you can perform exercises to improve your ability to detect fallacies. Metaphors help by training your brain to find the meaning hidden behind cleverly worded statements. You can also use your knowledge of logical fallacies to detect when someone is trying to hide something from you or influence your decision in a certain direction.

The "why" model

The whole point of being a leader is to inspire your employees to want to do what you want them to do. This is the definition of true power: making people want to bend to your will. This power is held in high regard because one, it is hard to wield it, and two, it is altruistic in nature. People are self-serving. The only way they would want to bend to anyone else's will is if they stand to benefit from it. The "why" model is the best strategy of thinking as a leader because it teaches you to wield this power.

With the "why" model, you will have to communicate your message precisely and articulately. You show your employees reasons why your vision is the best way forward for them and the company and in this way enforce their inner purpose and align it with your own. Few people can do something without a clear justification. You don't need people who do whatever you ask without asking why. In most cases, these people will do nothing at all unless you push them.

The "why" model was adopted into NLP during the NLPt era, which was also the time when psychotherapy was rising in prominence as a valid treatment for psychological issues. Its use on a personal level entails asking the question of why for every out-of-the-ordinary behavior till you reach the root cause. This is the one true way to resolve deep-seated issues and free yourself from self-sabotage.

Pavlovian Association

The Pavlovian Association Theory simply reiterates the concept we stated at the beginning, that thoughts and memories have sensory associations. This theory of thought is as much a strategy to employ in motivating yourself as it is a cautionary tale. You see, Ivan Pavlov (author of the Pavlovian association theory) conducted experiments that showed that human beings are extremely susceptible to classical conditioning. We create biological and mental associations at both the conscious and unconscious levels. Being aware of the associations you have made over the years means that you can free yourself from possible manipulation. On the other hand, you can exploit habits you already have to create new ones by creating associations.

Cognitive dissonance

Cognitive dissonance exists when people act contrary to their values, ideals, or beliefs. To make the actions logically palatable, we form new standards to fit them. A cognitive dissonance is a form of fallacy, except that it is internal and instead of changing the behavior to match the principle, we twist the principle around to accommodate our own failings. With NLP, we use mental maps to open the lid on our own unreasonable behavior and thus ensure that our beliefs and actions align.

The swish technique for negative thoughts

The swish technique is specially crafted to help us overcome irrational negative thoughts. We do this by changing the direction of our thoughts away from negativity and into positive territory. The swish technique is especially suited for this role because it leaves a trail for all our thoughts to follow, meaning that changing the direction of one negative thought from negative to positive induces all other thoughts we have to follow the same pattern.

The swish pattern cleans negative thoughts through the following process:

1. Detect a negative or unwanted thought and the bad feeling it stirs up

2. Separate the bad feeling from the thought-through focus. You might need to close your eyes or hum a funny lullaby here.

3. Search your mind for a replacement thought and shift your conscious mind from the negative feeling to the new positive thought.

4. Realize that you don't need to do anything because the negative thought has already been banished.

Problem-solving

As a common employee, you learned to pass the buck over to your manager. He or she was there to handle any unforeseen difficulties and smooth things over for you to do your job. Well, you are now the manager and it falls on you to bail out everyone who works under you. And when you form an audacious dream, you can expect to solve even more problems because there will be more difficulties arising. You can either look at problems as hindrances to your progress or as stepping-stones to a higher stage. All the successful business leaders of today (and ever) have followed the latter path, so that's what we will discuss in this section.

Adapting to your new role can be a problem in and of itself. When you are faced with an unfavorable situation, the mind perceives danger and activates the fight-or-flight instinct. When your body prepares for an emergency, blood stops flowing to the brain and is instead directed to motion muscles and organs. If you have ever been faced by a problem only to find a perfect solution long after the crisis has passed, this is probably because you made a decision in an instant of fight-or-flight adrenaline, and your brain was not fully powered to evaluate the options.

Thinking backwards

When you are faced with a problem, you will probably feel that your vision is challenged and your chances at future success are dimmed. This is especially true when you are following a strict timeline. A small problem could have serious repercussions down the line. Thinking about the future is a great idea at all times, except when you are trying to solve a problem. At this time and this time only, thinking backward holds the answers. It doesn't solve the problem, and the solution does not really come from the backward thinking, but it grounds you firmly enough that you can find the inner strength to deal with the problem.

Ultimately, what helps you solve a problem without losing your mind is deconstructing the problem, figuring out the expected outcomes, and accepting that they are inescapable. After that, you factor the problem into the future plan and go ahead accomplishing what you set off to accomplish.

This NLP technique of inversion, embracing problems, and making them part of the storyline is best embodied by Elon Musk. Elon is an entrepreneur who has encountered numerous problems in his career, from getting fired from his own company to losing millions of dollars' worth of NASA supplies. Despite the challenges, he powers forward and never wavers from his chosen path.

Entropy

Entropy is a philosophical principle that postulates that chaos is inevitable. However, much we try to prevent problems, they will always persist because no system can ever be maintained in a chaos-free state. This is an important principle for managers to understand, especially when they are dealing with problems at the workplace. Not every tiny problem will require your personal interference.

More importantly, you must not worry about small problems. Most people feel indicted by problems that arise in their department. This could never be further from the truth, as indicated by the entropy principle. The sooner you realize this, the sooner you can stop worrying and beating yourself up when things don't go according to plan.

To the extent that they don't disrupt much or disrupt you from pursuing your vision (micro problems) embrace the chaos and let it motivate you. As for any other sort of disruption, you must dedicate yourself to beating back disruptions from every area of your life. The way to do this is to be disciplined, conscientious, and methodical planners.

NLP Exercise to overcome entropy

1. Embrace the mental model of entropy; life is designed to resort to a disorderly fashion. You cannot control the future or anything that happens in the present.

2. Clean up your room; just because the world resorts to disorder does not mean you let disorder take over.

3. Adopt orderliness.

4. Determine what you can do for the community and do it.

5. Practice consciousness in everything you do.

First and second-order change

Every action we do has consequences beyond the immediate result. When you manage to stop a valuable employee from quitting by offering him or her a generous pay raise, you will have to deal with other employees who may feel that they deserve a raise as well. You will also give the impression that people can get their way with you by holding you hostage to ransom. These are the second-order consequences that every leader must consider when solving a problem.

When using NLP techniques like the swish pattern to change negative thoughts or habits, we use the conscious, not unconscious, parts of the mind. This means that unconsciously, parts of the mind that were associated with the old habits are left untouched. If you don't account for the second-order changes that the unconscious will demand, the habits changed will simply be replaced with new ones. For example, knuckle crackers who use a swish pattern to change their behavior to flexing their fingers would soon realize that they can crack other parts of their bodies to derive the same satisfaction they got from cracking their knuckles.

As a business leader, it falls on you to keep in mind the second-order consequences of your actions, especially when solving problems. The best way to do this is to find the root causes of a problem and endeavor to change that instead of treating the symptoms. In our example above, instead of rewarding a salary raise, you should figure out exactly what the employee needs. Sometimes appreciation is more important than money and making your best employees feel appreciated goes a long way. By simply thinking about the consequences of the actions you do to solve a problem, you will prevent a lot more problems from following in the wake and conserve a lot of your resources.

Reframing

NLP principles teach that the most constructive thing to do when faced with a problem is to use reframing to get a positive spin on the problem. This reduces the distress to our brains and dims the fight-or-flight response that is responsible for that mind-numbing freeze-reflex when faced with a problem. Instead of thinking what an inconvenience a problem creates for you, try and think about the mental and character strength you will reap from solving it.

Reframing can entail changing the perspective on the angle from which you look at a problem or the seriousness of a problem. To deal with the latter, you simply break the challenge down into smaller pieces. These will be easier to deal with. And while you are at it, coming up with a solution to the smaller problems (which is easier) will embolden you to deal with the bigger challenge, however big it seems.

By combining NLP with willpower exercises, you will embolden yourself to move away from the problem and focus on the solution. The recommended time allocation is 20% on the problem, getting all the facts right and considering the implications, and 80% on the solution.

Anticipation

When making plans, you are required to use NLP's future pacing to visualize the outcome to motivate yourself to pursue it tirelessly. When you are a leader, the visualization must take into account possible issues that may arise during the implementation of action plans. This is called anticipation. It helps you prepare in advance for challenges and have an idea of how the problems could be mitigated. Essentially, anticipation entails answering the question, "What could possibly go wrong?"

Anticipation does not just help you solve the problem; it also helps you anticipate them and put in place measures to ensure that the problems never arise in the first place. To do this, you must start with a thorough breakdown of all the tasks and activities you associated with the project. Answer the following questions:

- Are there any weaknesses and if there are, what are they?

- Is the plan foolproof?

- What specific areas present a possible risk?
- What is the cost of risk occurrence?
- What can be done to stop the problems before they arise?

Not only does anticipation help you avoid risks, but it also helps you to limit any possible damage they might cause.

The "what" model

When you ask the question "why" about a problem, you get to its cause. When searching for the solution, however, the starting point should be "what," not "why." This way, you stop looking for a reason why something happened and simply find a solution. It is an important strategy, especially when you don't have as much time to spend finding the root cause of a problem. However, asking what you can do about a problem rather than why things are going wrong has other advantages. It opens your mind up to finding solutions instead of challenging your whole system for causing a problem.

Next time you are faced with a real problem at work, ask the following five questions about the solution you formulate:

- What would (insert role model) do to solve a problem like this?
- What explanation can I give for choosing this particular solution and not any other?
- What am I trying to achieve with this solution?
- What will I think about the solution I came up with within 10 years?
- What information am I relying on to justify the solution?

These questions give you perspective and take you out of your comfort zone, allowing you to examine a serious problem with a fresh outlook.

NLP problem-solving exercise

- Review the history of the problem you are trying to solve. Write down a detailed description.

- Using the NLP technique of well-formed outcome, imagine that you have already solved the problem.

- Think of everything you can do to solve the problem. Brainstorm as many solutions as possible.

- Settle on the most suitable solution and focus keenly on it.

- Let the realization that you can solve the problem wash through you, relaxing you. There is no reason to worry, you got this!

- Close your eyes and visualize the problem being solved.

- Your inner mind will continue to work on the problem in the most fulfilling way. This could go on for up to half an hour.

- You will start feeling the urge to move when your mind has resolved the problem. Most of the time, you will come out of the exercise with a strong urge to do something about your problem.

- Create an action plan for the duration it will take you to solve the problem, detailing the steps you will need to take.

- Follow the action plan strictly to ensure that you get the outcome you desired.

Decision making

Decision making uses all the concepts discussed in thinking and problem solving to formulate the most appropriate course of action for your department to achieve its goals. While problem-solving can be about a range of issues and concerns, decision making is more specifically concerned with the long-term end result.

When making any decision, you must keep the vision in mind. In fact, the vision is the single most influential consideration in decision making. Only those decisions that will further the strategic cause of the organization are worth making. In this section, we will look at the approaches to decision making that a good leader must follow.

Confirmation bias

Let's discuss first things first and start with the biggest hindrance to decision making. Confirmation bias is a sort of fallacy that blinds us to all information but that which supports our views. In decision making, people are very likely to notice and acknowledge information supporting a decision they already made. In the same vein, any information that is contrary to a decision will be dismissed. So, if you decide to venture into a new area and diversify, you will be more likely to find evidence supporting the concepts of diversification. Even though the risks are still there, your confirmation bias will lead to you glossing over them.

Obviously, this is a very dangerous trap to be caught in. If you cannot identify or acknowledge evidence pointing to mistakes you have made in a decision, this could have disastrous consequences not just for you but also for the whole company.

Even more worrisome is the fact that human beings tend to form an opinion about things really fast. Confirmation bias does not just affect the decisions you have already made. It influences the ones you make. So, if you are more inclined to an idea or a solution, you will gravitate towards evidence that points towards its suitability. If you don't check this inclination, you risk making decisions based on personal rather than business considerations. These decisions will obviously be flawed and will be more likely to bring about even more problems.

NLP decision-making process

Luckily, you can make good and unbiased decisions using the concepts of neuro-linguistic programming. NLP strategies present the master key to effective outcomes for every decision that you make.

Begin with the end in mind: The main reason why confirmation bias distorts your decision making is that you have a personal opinion about the decision. The problem arises when your problem is not backed by the facts.

However, if you can start by considering existing information, both quantitative and qualitative, you increase the chances of your decision is based on good information and factual reasoning. Henceforth, your personally preferred decision will be based on objective information and cannot thus be fallacious. In fact, by beginning with the end in mind and using factual information to verify it, you pave the way for your instinct to kick in and guide you towards the ideal decision.

But as much as your decisions affect the whole group you lead, it is also a personal victory for you when you make a winning decision. So, visualize the outcome of the decision you are about to make and see, hear, and feel it. If it is a good feeling, go for it. But if a big part of the outcome doesn't look or feel good, abandon the idea at once.

1. Elicit values/vision: in the event that you have already created the vision and mission statement for your division, making decisions is simply a matter of consulting the vision statement and considering the impact of your decision on the attainment of the same. Why is it important that you get the outcome your current decision will bring? Can you do without it? How essential is it that you make the decision? How urgent?

2. Activate the desire to achieve: making a decision is not just a matter of choosing to do something. It is also a commitment you make to pursue a particular aim to the end. In this step of the decision-making process using NLP, you must increase your determination to get to the desired outcome. Part of this entails visualizing the outcome as a picture and enhancing your vision of it to all the senses. Smell it, taste it, see it in your mind, and feel the thrill of victory. This is your outcome picture and you should be able to recall it anytime you need to motivate yourself to pursue the desired outcome.

3. Keep the timeline in mind: every good outcome must be timed. So, when you make the decision to pursue a particular end, make the decision as specific about the timeline as possible. For example, if you decide to diversify into new markets, a more effective way to make the decision is to say, "Diversify into new markets within the next two years." When you hold yourself to a specific timeline, you become more accountable and thus more driven to achieve.

Decision making and self-awareness

Perfect decision-making capabilities are almost exclusively a preserve of highly driven people. Studies have found that personality plays a major role in the decision-making process. One of the most important aspects of personality that affects decision making is self-awareness. When you are self-aware, you know exactly what you want to achieve in a week, a month, a year, and ten years from now. You also know your limitations and capabilities.

The former allows you to make decisions faster because you simply ask yourself "How does this decision get me closer to my ultimate goal?" People who go through life without any set pursuit or goals don't just make bad decisions. Sometimes they avoid making them altogether by avoiding situations that might require them to choose. If you habitually struggle to make decisions, your sense of self is the first place you should go to look for a solution.

Having no awareness of our capabilities also brings about doubts. When you doubt yourself, you open the door for insecurities to ram you down and erode your decision-making capabilities. So, if your decision-making capabilities have been hampered since you earned that promotion, it is high time you analyze the real emotions you harbor about it. Sometimes you could be avoiding making decisions because you don't feel qualified to make such big choices. For improved decision-making capabilities, increase your self-worth.

Modeling

When working to improve our decision-making capabilities, we use two similar NLP techniques: metamodeling and modeling. Metamodeling is the practice of observing and understanding our own mental models and ways of doing things. It also doubles up as the easiest way to identify personal limitations that could be hindering the attainment of our utmost desires. We use it to find out ways through which we have been hampering our own success. And by employing the concepts of modeling discussed in chapter 1, we are able to replace the constraints that stop us from making good decisions with concepts borrowed from the best business leaders.

In metamodeling, observe your reaction to decision making. What goes through your mind when an opportunity to make a big decision comes by? Are you invigorated or frightened? If your reaction is negative, what could be causing this? You must reach a position of being comfortable making huge decisions.

While observing your thought patterns, it is important to pay attention to the negative patterns of generalization, distortion, cause-effect statements, and cherry-picking. With generalization, you form a universal statement based on an observation of a few events. Distortions happen when you read people or situations wrong and make erroneous interpretations. Sometimes setting a high goal and not meeting it might lead to a rebuke from your boss. Hardly will you ever get fired for going out of your way and failing unless you were targeted for the sack anyway. But a common impediment to decision making, especially of the strategic kind, is the cause-effect idea that you might get fired if you fail. Finally, cherry-picking is the mental model that powers all the thought patterns listed above. It allows you to ignore all evidence contrary to your distortion, generalization, or wrong cause-effect association and blow up the supporting evidence.

After identifying your shortcomings in decision making, you must then find an outstanding business leader with excellent decision-making ability and copy their practices. These include business leaders like Lee Iacocca, Bill Gates, Anthony Robbins, and Steve Jobs among others. Below, we discuss the common decision-making habits the outstanding leaders listed above exhibit that you can model.

NLP exercises for decision making

When you use NLP in your decision-making process, you must incorporate the visual, auditory, and kinesthetic senses. But more specifically, some of the most effective NLP practices for decision making include:

Recognize the reality

You must understand perfectly the options available for you to choose from. Some minor issues might be misconstrued as problems until you actually evaluate them.

Understand your options

A dilemma may turn out to be anything but, as soon as you articulate the options. This is why some people use a pros-and-cons list to make decisions. It allows you to actually think about the different reasons why you might want to make a particular option. While evaluating the options, be sure to keep your eyes on the big picture. As the saying goes, "Don't step over a dollar to pick a dime."

Trust your gut

Decisions can either be supported by rigorously analyzed data or it can be sensed by the heart. While it is not 100 percent reliable, instinct is a very powerful asset for decision-makers. It relies on unconscious information to come up with a decision that you can feel but not necessarily explain.

Have an alternate plan

While some people believe that having a plan B is rooting for plan A to fail, successful leaders call this common sense. Because failure is unavoidable, the only way to insure yourself from massive losses is to have an alternative in the event that your first idea does not initially work out. Even if, in the way of Elon Musk, your plan is to start all over again, you must be willing to carry on when things do not initially work out as you planned.

Chapter 4: Productivity and time management

As a leader, you want to make the most efficient use of your time and boost productivity. This is the measure that employers and observers everywhere use to determine your ability to lead. To attain the highest levels of productivity possible, you must be skilled at time management. These two skills go hand in hand. Time management influences productivity and high productivity inspires better time management. In this chapter, we will evaluate both using NLP techniques.

Personal productivity

Ultimately, your success as a leader will be judged by the level of productivity you will achieve. This judgment will be made based on the performance of your whole team, but it will be driven more by your ability to attain high rewards using the least possible resources. On a personal level, productivity can be achieved by adhering to NLP processes like the four-step process known as PDCA (plan, do, check, adjust), removing distractions, overcoming procrastination, and understanding how the brain works.

PDCA

The PDCA cycle of productivity is an interactive strategy for continuous self-improvement and the resolution of challenges to productivity. It was created in 1950 by Dr. William Edward Deming to help business managers refine their project delivery processes and has been adopted into NLP to help people increase their personal productivity.

Plan

The awareness of what you are working for is very crucial for productivity. If you don't have a good idea of what goals you want to reach, chances are you will spend your time flitting from one task to another without ever getting anything done. At best, you will achieve moderate success. But if you really want to be a roaring success, you must have a coherent plan of how to get where you intend to get to. The best way to devise a plan is to make it SMART for reasons discussed further below.

Do

The only way to ever be productive is to actually do something. You must be willing to do the things you need to do to reach your goal. Breaking down an objective into smaller tasks is one way to simplify the accomplishment of goals.

Check

Unless you monitor your progress, you can never be sure if you are actually getting anything done. In making smart goals, the M stands for measurable. Your productivity must be measurable. How many new clients per month is good enough? What is the ideal amount of time to spend bringing them in? What percentage of growth in sales or profit is acceptable? All these are quantifiable measurements that you can track.

To ensure that you are on course to reach your goal, check up on your own progress every once in a while. The closer you get to your goal, the more motivated you will feel about doing the work you do.

Adjust

If you have been working hard but not getting anywhere on your goals, it might be time to change your behavior. You are supposed to act on the observations you make about your own work. If you have been doing well, give yourself a reward. If you are not getting closer to your goal, consider adopting a different approach.

Eliminate distractions

Even though our brains can only process about nine bits of information at a time, our brains process up to two billion bits in the conscious and unconscious mind. The distractions that hamper our productivity could be as small as annoying noises, the unsuitable temperature in our place of work, or an uncomfortable chair or desk. Distractions grow in size up to social media and unresolved personal issues, including psychological ones like lack of self-belief, among others.

You should eliminate as many of the distractions you know as possible to give your mind the chance to focus on the most important tasks. Environmental distractions like the hot or cold room can be eliminated simply enough, but dealing with psychological distractions is a little more complicated.

NLP exercises for personal productivity

But by using NLP, it is possible to create an environment where you can still get some good work done despite the mental distractions. This can be done using visualization exercises or anchors.

Anchoring exercise:

- Take note of your environment every time you are in a very productive state.

- Come up with a phrase that captures this moment or a gesture (or both).

- Perform the gesture or say the phrase every time you are in the zone of high productivity.

- Use the phrase or gesture to get yourself into a state of high productivity when you are feeling lethargic.

Visualization exercise:

This is something to do every morning as soon as you get to your office. It sets you up for high productivity through the day.

- Close your eyes.

- Visualize a time when you were at your most productive.

- Let the image consume your senses and give yourself up to this feeling of success.

- See yourself being this productive throughout the day.

- Be productive throughout the day.

Take breaks

The brain is capable of working for a maximum of 90 minutes at a time when you keep distractions to a minimum. Limiting your work sessions to 90 minutes at a time can be a way to attain massive productivity because it gives your brain time to refresh. The breaks present you with the perfect opportunity to network and observe the work environment. If you have spent the first 90 minutes of the day in a meeting, try to spend the next session doing something else. This rotation of tasks ensures that your mind never tires and will always be productive as ever in every new session.

Avoid procrastination

Above anything else we might discuss here, the ability to put off short-term gain for long-term benefits determines your level of productivity and ultimately your success. The only problem with this is that people derive greater pleasure from short-term indulgences. We are biologically engineered to gravitate towards them. However, you can still get the satisfaction of short-term indulgences from doing long-term stuff. This NLP practice utilizes positive reinforcement and reward systems to motivate the highest levels of productivity and satisfaction from work that is ordinarily tedious and monotonous. If keeping on top of your inbox is something you struggle with, give yourself a reward after replying to every email and reading every important message. You will start to associate the task with the satisfaction you get from the reward and be more inclined to do it.

Workplace productivity

When you are the leader, the productivity of the team you are in charge of determines your own success. And while it might be challenging to motivate everyone in your team to pursue success or selflessly commit to the group effort, you can use NLP to turn around any negative attitudes that derail work, inspire employees to change bad habits, and improve the general productivity of everybody in your team.

Set objectives

A common objective in the workplace improves productivity by pooling resources together. A common objective directs the team towards a single purpose, with employees working harder to deliver. See, most of the time people don't fail to achieve success because they are incapable. It is simply a matter of not understanding what is expected of them.

When you set an objective for the whole team to pursue, you should make sure that you assign tasks to each and every employee. This way, they will recognize their role in the whole process and work harder knowing that their success is the success of the whole group, which is their success. Follow that? If an employee succeeds, the whole group succeeds; if the whole group succeeds, the employee succeeds. The failure of a single employee in a team effort leads to double failure and their success to double success.

Boost morale

The only way employees will recognize and appreciate their role in the success of the whole team is when they are motivated to excel. To succeed in leadership, you must consider the morale of your employees. Why should you bother? Well, because unmotivated employees will frustrate your best efforts at productivity. That's why.

You can use team-building exercises to foster a spirit of togetherness, but more importantly, you must consider your employees' personal dreams and objectives. Failure to account for the goals of employees will result in feelings of alienation, poor motivation, and possibly sabotage.

Communication

Communication is the foundation of every strong relationship. To get the best out of your team, you should improve the way you talk with them and how you communicate your goals and objectives. This you must do with all players involved in your workplace, from subordinates to bosses and outsourcing partners. If communication between you and any partner breaks down, the consequences will be felt across the board.

Improved delegation

Delegation is one of the most important tools in your managerial toolbox for improving productivity. This strategy might appear like something that improves your own productivity more than that of the team. But in a real sense, delegating does more to boost the productivity of your employees. It gives them the sense that they are part of the team and can be counted on to play an important part. Of course, you must know the difference between delegating and shoving off your work on the most eager employee. It only builds resentment in the long run and does nothing whatsoever to improve your productivity or that of your team.

Learning and development

To improve the productivity of your team, you must perfect the art of bringing out the abilities of your employees. By using NLP, you can unlock the wealth of potential and knowledge in every one of your employees and make the most of them to boost the productivity of the whole team. By teaching employees the NLP techniques for unlocking their potential, you empower them to take charge of their careers and to be more proactive. Proactive employees do more to bring success to the whole team and serve as an example to others.

Change bad attitudes

If your team has a bad attitude to work, chances are you are not responsible for that since you are new. Bad attitudes at the workplace develop when managers neglect the psychological needs of employees. Overworking is one chief cause of bad attitudes. Mismanagement, poor communication, favoritism, and lack of direction are other causes of bad attitudes. To reverse the harm done by poor leadership, teach employees to recognize their own role in their work-life balance and satisfaction, then work with them to create a nurturing environment.

Finding the state of flow

The peak of productivity is reached when you get in the state of flow. Here, the demands of the activity at hand consume all our attention, skills, and awareness. When you get in the state of flow, you can achieve astounding levels of efficiency and the ability to accomplish tasks that are otherwise challenging. To achieve the state of flow, our highest, purpose-driven goals have to be aligned with the smaller task-driven goals. For example, you can say that you are in flow when you manage to reach the target number of new clients in a week while working towards the higher aim of doubling sales or profit for the year.

Other than boosting productivity, being in the state of flow allows us to grow as individuals as well as with the team. While it is not entirely impossible to get in a state of flow alone, it is always so much better when the results you get are earned by a team effort. And even though happiness is not the foremost emotion you will be feeling while in the zone, you will experience massive growth afterwards. You will also find the whole experience fulfilling and extremely addictive. And if you can manage to get your whole team addicted to extreme productivity, then your quest for success as a leader is already half won!

NLP exercises to get into a flow

The state of flow sure does sound like the ideal workplace atmosphere to have, doesn't it? A state where productivity is boosted to the highest levels, not just for you but your whole team, is the ideal situation for any manager to find him or herself in. So, how exactly can you whip up your team into a state of flow and consistently hit your targets and achieve your goals? Well, NLP has got you covered!

The most important NLP exercises to get into the state of flow are anchoring, visualization, and reframing. The anchor conditions your mind to go back to previous moments of high productivity and visualization excites you to work towards the desired outcome.

1. First off, you must create a vision for your team and ensure that every member is fully committed to it.

2. Before starting the day, gather your team around and guide them through a visualization exercise envisioning a future when you will have achieved the vision.

3. Create a catchphrase to start every meeting with to create a deeper connection to the team for every member.

4. Whenever you achieve a goal, bring the team together for a reward like champagne, cake, or whatever every member likes. A reward, especially one that is enjoyed together, fosters teamwork and creates an anchor for success.

5. Be sure to make a toast to your team's success, invoking the catchphrase you have created for it. This further strengthens the

anchor your team has towards collective success.

6. Respond to concerns, both personal and professional, of all your team members. This is very important to avoid disharmony when some members fall out of touch with the rest of the team.

Reframing comes in handy when you turn out to be unsuccessful. And the chances are high that you will face failure at one time or another, regardless of you and your team's commitment to the goals. You must lead your team in reframing any undesirable events, whether you will pivot in another direction and develop strategies or change strategies and carry on as before. When dealing with failure:

1. Recognize the failure in all its scope. Be as specific as possible and put things in perspective. For example, the failure to meet a target of 50% growth in sales is not as big if you got to 30% growth.

2. Find out why you failed in your quest. Was it too high? Did the team break down? List all the factors that led to the failure.

3. Rationalize. If you failed to reach the target because it was too high, you might want to

scale it down a bit. If you do this, remember to celebrate the small victory to keep morale high. Sometimes teams fall apart not because they failed, but because they did not meet a high goal. Even though technically they succeeded, failing to celebrate the success, even underwhelming as it was, led to demoralization and worse, failure.

4. Celebrate the small wins. A small win celebrated is more motivational than a big win that is not.

Time management

You only have so many hours to do what you need to do every day. If you don't plan your time properly, you will end up spending all your time on the unimportant things and having no time for what really matters. Of all the resources we have, time is the most valuable. You can get more money, learn new skills or hire people with them, you can learn new things and become knowledgeable, but you can never get more of a valuable resource called time. When a day goes by, it is gone forever and can never be recovered. If you made proper use of it, it will leave you enriched. Fail to maximize the opportunities that come to you throughout the day and they are gone, possibly forever. The value of every minute, every hour, and every day comes from the things you accomplish and the demands that are made of you.

And as a leader, you will be required to do more every hour of the day. Not only must you get the most out of YOU, it falls on you to ensure that your whole team performs at optimal levels. In this section, we will look at time management at the personal and team levels.

NLP Time management strategies

On a personal level, the proper use of time will be determined by several factors including your sense of direction, creating focus areas, milestone checking, and developing skills.

The proper understanding of long-term goals is very important for time management. It determines the amount of time we allocate to the most important activities. These important activities become our focus area, places where we dedicate most of our energies and time. Focus areas are supposed to be the activities that play the biggest part in getting us to the long-term goals.

These activities are demarcated using milestones, which allow you to verify your progress along the way. Only by tracking progress can you know when or if you need to up your game. And whether or not you need to up your game to achieve your goals, skills development comes naturally with the pursuit of personal goals. Your ability to accomplish a particular task increases in direct proportion to the amount of time you spend doing it. Ultimately, you find that you need less time to do the same amount of work overtime.

To ensure that you manage your time in the best way possible for maximum yields, the following seven strategies will come in handy.

Set your priorities right

The best strategy to set your activity of main concern is to leaf through your vision statement and determine which three activities will bring you closest to the target. You should then figure out how much time your focus should remain on the activities before moving on to the next step. When your priority activities are clear, your time allocation becomes clear also, mostly because you are able to give precedent to the most important tasks even when the demands on your time are overwhelming.

Build your energy

Energy is another resource that we have in limited quantities. You start with a full tank of energy in the morning and use it up until you are running on empty by nighttime. The only difference between time and energy resources is that you can increase the amount of energy you have at the beginning of the day by resting properly, exercising, and proper dieting. Emotional energy can also be boosted by visualization exercises and meditating, ultimately building your focus, energy, and effectiveness. More energy means that you get more out of your day every day which is the ultimate goal of time management.

Establish a routine

It takes quite a lot of energy and time to start a new routine, but maintaining a routine is the least time-consuming activity ever. The most important routines for good time management are the morning and evening (sleeping) routines. They are especially important because they boost not just your ability to manage your time but also the capacity to get the most out of it.

Make the diary your best friend

A diary is an ultimate tool for the budgeting of time use. But every other manager can schedule their activities in their diary and manage their time just fine. When you use NLP time-management strategies, you pay special attention to hotspots in your diary and plan to do certain activities at the times most suitable to do them.

You see, all hours of your day are not equal. Some are suited for difficult tasks and some are best suited for relaxation. To note these different times of the day, you must practice full awareness during the day. Notice how you feel in the morning, midmorning, early afternoon, and the evening. When do you feel most alert? At what times is your brain sleepy and lethargic? Schedule intellectually demanding tasks when your mind is at its sharpest and engage in more physical activities when your mind is less sharp—activities that involve movement, for example.

Ask yourself a question... or two

Time management does not just happen by accident. It is something we do consciously by ensuring that we make the most out of every hour throughout the day. Questioning the time used for tasks and activities increases the value we place on time and fosters better time management. Questioning your time allocation for tasks allows you to keep improving on both the time allocation and task accomplishment.

Ready, set, go!

The most important time to mark when doing something is the start and finish times. You must start every activity you intend to finish and you must finish everything you start. Observe this rule and you will increase the utility of your time every single day. In between the starting and the finishing line, you must pace yourself. A steady pace with occasional sprints is the best strategy, especially for tasks that require a lot of time to get done.

Create a structure

We form habits because we do something over and over again and derive a measure of pleasure from it. However, there is another strategy to form habits: creating a structure of actions. A structured workday ensures that you have specific times for doing the most important things like eating, sleeping, exercising, and working. Every activity should be scheduled with strict timelines to reinforce the need for you to do them at the right time.

The 4 Ds

In a more simplified manner, you can manage your time by adhering to the 4 Ds of time management. The 4 Ds of time management is a way to help you put your time to the best use by determining how you handle tasks. It classifies tasks into four groups, namely: the ones you delete, the ones you delegate, the ones you do, and the ones you defer.

Tasks to delete

As a leader, you should only give your attention to the tasks that are absolutely necessary. If an activity does not really help you get closer to your ultimate goal, then you must strike it off your list of to-dos. To determine the activities that are not worthwhile and that are best deleted, use the Pareto 80/20 rule. See, in most cases, 80% of what we do only brings 20% of the benefits. Activities that fall in this bulk category can be deleted with little to no negative impact on our productivity but with massive amounts of time freed for more productive work.

Tasks to delegate

As the team leader, you will be responsible for the management of time at the workplace, especially for projects. In the course of your day, you will be put in a position where you must decide whether or not an activity is important enough to tackle right away or tackle it at all. You will also have to prioritize between activities happening simultaneously, like a meeting with an old client and an interview with a prospective one. When this happens, you must pick one activity to place your focus on and hand over the less important task to your subordinates. However, don't completely abdicate by handing out any difficult task and washing your hands of it. Only hand over the tasks you must and follow up to ensure that whoever does it meets the quality standards.

Tasks to do right away

Any important task is a task worth doing straight away. With "do it," I mean that you must follow up on the task to completion. The biggest mistake people make is to start a task then leave it halfway through and start doing something else. By the end of the day, you will have started to do, but not completed, so many tasks it will be difficult to gauge your level of success. Ultimately, the numerous task folders open in your mind will leave you feeling stressed and anxious. Don't get trapped in the paper-shuffling trap. Finish every task you start as soon as possible then move on to the next thing.

Tasks to defer

Obviously, as you go through your to-do list, you must prioritize some tasks over others. This means that you will have to put aside some other tasks for some other time. These are the tasks that are important but not as urgent, so they can be delayed without affecting the ultimate goal.

The best way to classify tasks into the 4 Ds is by going through your to-do list each morning and using the Eisenhower Matrix to group your tasks. You must do the urgent and important tasks, delegate the urgent but not important ones, defer the important but not urgent ones, and delete tasks that are neither urgent nor important.

Chapter 5: Communication, negotiation, and presentation

Communication and interpersonal relationships are critical components of neuro-linguistic programming. They also play a big part in the professional work of a manager, because a lot of what you will be doing will be coordinating the efforts of various stakeholders to achieve a specific goal. In this chapter, we will look at the role that communication, negotiation, and presentation play in the makings of a great business leader.

Communication

One skill that you must develop to a high standard as a leader is the ability to communicate clearly, convincingly, and consistently. The vision you develop for your team (which we have said several times is a very stabilizing force to your leadership) can only be realized if you convey it in an effective manner.

This is the conventional view of communication and its relevance to leadership. However, with NLP, we know that communication goes beyond the words you say to your employees or clients to the way you absorb and process ideas and information from the world. In this section, we will look at all the ways that leaders communicate and how you can enhance your communication for success in your management career.

Communication filters

All forms of communication take place in five channels, namely: visual, auditory, kinesthetic (feelings, touch, pressure), olfactory (smell), and gustatory (taste). These input channels make up the communication model used in NLP to help us absorb, process, and react to information from the environment including what other people say, do, and how they look, as well as the environment where the communication takes place. However, the ultimate information that reaches us is determined not by the other person or the environment but our own filters. These filters delete, distort, and generalize information from the outer world and could impact in a big way how we deal with the rest of the world.

In deleting, our input channels omit some parts of the messages absorbed from the world and leave only the important or useful bits or whatever we perceive to be the most important bits. One instance where deletion occurs is when we use a phone and drive at the same time. The visual channels are overpowered by the information that needs to be absorbed, resulting in poor performance in both.

Distortion occurs when we misrepresent the information we absorb to create different meanings than what they actually give. On one hand, distortion can be a powerful motivational tool that can help us create a rosy future for ourselves in our minds. When we do this with enough conviction, we can create powerful visualizations.

On the other hand, distorting information can lead to serious misunderstandings. If you don't know what someone means when they do or say something, it is best to wait till you have gathered enough information before interpreting their actions or words. This saves you from potential misunderstandings which can be catastrophic when you are a manager charged with offering leadership and guidance.

Generalization is a breakdown in interpretation that happens when you draw universal conclusions based on a single experience. This leads to stereotypical thinking that could be very dangerous and interfere with your ability to lead. Information should be interpreted as independent of past experiences.

Intrapersonal communication

One of the many definitions of communication is simply "the means of transmitting or receiving ideas or feelings." Most people believe that communication only occurs when there is a direct exchange of information between two people, but in truth, communication takes place even when we receive and decode information from our environment. On the one hand, you must understand that your brain is always collecting information from all around you. Our thinking and decision making are influenced by both the information we perceive consciously and that which reaches our minds at the unconscious level. Being aware of the power of these unconscious communication pathways can boost your effectiveness as a manager.

The things you say to yourself also count as a form of communication because they entail the exchange of information between the conscious and the unconscious parts of our minds. These forms of information exchange are known as intrapersonal communication and they entail planning, calculating, internal monologue, and daydreaming. Using NLP, you can enhance the use of internal monologue and daydreaming to impact your mind with greater productivity.

Internal monologue includes the things you say to yourself about yourself, the things you do, and things that happen around you. Listening to your internal monologue is one way of examining your own psyche to determine the state of your mind. And because it is a window into your unconscious mind, you can also exploit internal monologue to impart yourself with positive and inspirational messages.

Chanting is one positive way of imparting positive messages into your mind. Consistently saying something about and to yourself eventually tricks your brain into believing it. As a new manager, you might need to utilize the gift of chanting to lift your confidence in your ability to take on the duties of your job with confidence and do so to great success.

Simply mattering things like "you got this" under your breath can calm you in a tense situation.

When you do it over time, your mind takes in the message and starts to act it out. This means that you will find yourself actually being in control of situations, however stressful, without losing your mind. All because you said it to yourself and you believed it.

Daydreaming is an unconscious means of communication that you can use to enhance your skills as a manager. Any time you are daydreaming is a time when you transport yourself into an ideal future situation. This communicates your deepest desires, which is why you mostly find yourself daydreaming when you are excited about something. The only problem with most people is that they daydream without purpose. It is something they do when bored and needing an escape. By doing it with intent and committing your mind to the process, you can convert daydreaming to future pacing and use it not just to visualize a future with a prospective mate but also to visualize your successful future and goals.

Leadership communication

All the forms of communication that take place between managers and their subordinates, peers, and their seniors are called leadership communication. It is underlined by the need to convey the capacity to lead at all times. When communicating as a leader, you will see greater results if you make it grounded in your own vision as a leader and the organizational values. The culture and climate of the organization must shine through your communication.

Leadership communication models include significance, cadence, values, and consistency. Regardless of the perceptions of your employees, peers, or bosses have about you, these aspects will factor into their interpretation of whatever you say. This is especially true for official communication. Anything you say will be treated as significant, including a random compliment to an employee about the quality of their work. It is very important that you keep this in mind to avoid sending the wrong signals. And especially when communicating with your bosses, the values of the organization must shine through when you communicate. Your vision and mission statement plays an especially big part of your communication strategies as a leader.

In fact, affirming the vision you have created for your team and how it falls within the vision of the whole company is one of the most important purposes of leadership communication. With proper leadership and communication, junior leaders can even create a vision that shapes the whole organization. When General George C. Marshall was the Chief of Staff of the US Army during World War II, he created a plan for the entry of America into what most considered a European conflict. He then appeared in Congress several times to convey his opinion about the need for the country to mobilize and take an active part in the war. For his ability to communicate his vision for the military and convince his superiors (the president of the United States and Congress), he was rewarded with a five-star rank in the military, an appointment to the position of Secretary of State under President Harry S. Truman, and a Nobel Peace Prize award in 1953.

This is the power of good communication driving transformational initiatives. Without General Marshall, the United States Military would not have been able to mobilize the massive resources he secured to advance its defense and assault weapons systems and practically win World War II for the Allied forces.

Leadership communication also allows you to galvanize your employees, peers, and seniors to rally behind an initiative. This is important because it is impossible to achieve any worthwhile thing in business without the help of others. Even if you have the best proposal with great potential for profit to the company, you will probably see little support until you convince all the stakeholders to get behind you on it.

Another purpose of leadership communication is to coach your junior employees. Since they look up to you for leadership, any instructions coming from you will make them feel valued and seen. Sometimes that is all an employee needs. As for you, the coaching you do will pay you back with greater productivity and efficiency from employees who actually understand what is expected of them and who knows how to deliver. Even if you offer coaching through contracted professionals, it still speaks to your desire to see the people who work for you build their skills.

Finally, when you are a leader, communication is as much about talking as it is about listening. When you listen, you communicate volumes nonverbally, like the fact that you care about employee, peer, or senior input in your work. Communicating without expecting, asking for, or listening to feedback is destructive and is likely to result in an eventual breakdown.

The Milton model of communication

The Milton Model is an approach to communication that borrows from the language patterns of hypnotic communication. It was developed from the concepts of noted hypnotist Milton Erickson and is considered to be a method of accessing the covert elements of our personality through language-induced trances. From the Milton model, we have three other communication models: rapport, indirect communication, and unconscious interpersonal communication.

Rapport

We use the concepts of hypnosis to create a better model of exchanging ideas and responses to information. This is an important asset to have as a business leader because much of the communication you will be doing will be aimed at convincing people to do something they might not necessarily be willing to do. When you can make a person empathize with you, you will realize that more of what you say meet a positive response.

Using NLP principles, you should mirror the body language of your audience to tune into their world. This includes matching their body language, breathing, posture, and tone of voice. After mirroring their nonverbal cues, you occupy the same state of being with the person, with him or her being the object and you the reflection that copies their actions. However, you can take over and start leading by changing your behavior and gestures in a covert and dominant manner. Rapport is very effective when you are trying to sell an idea to a higher authority. Once you have established a rapport, they will be more likely to agree with your ideas. Not only that, the person will probably be eager to do so.

Indirect communication

This entails using the NLP technique of metaphors to gain access to the unconscious mind of a person. This way, you can implant ideas into a person's mind by giving them a metaphor with a correlation to what you want them to do. This is called an indirect suggestion. It is accomplished with the use of purposefully vague metaphors. See, it is harder to get someone, let's say your boss, to agree with you if you go to him or her and say, "We need to invest in this new technology. It will boost our bottom line."

But you could approach him or her and vaguely suggest that the bottom line is not as strong as it used to be, but this new technology is really paying off for the people who have invested in it. If you launch into a different topic, he or she might not even notice the metaphor. But the power of a metaphor is in the way it latches onto the unconscious. Don't be surprised if the next time you talk, he or she asks you to tell them more about the technology you mentioned. You may even ask for the opportunity to explain it with a PowerPoint presentation because, after all, he came to you! Indirect communication using metaphors can be a very useful resource when used the right way.

Unconscious interpersonal communication

This Miltonian NLP strategy uses ambiguous language and nonverbal communication to achieve almost the same results as indirect communication. The only difference is that this strategy uses blurred boundaries of meaning to distract the conscious mind rather than metaphors. The aim of unconscious communication is to give the unconscious mind the opportunity to shine through, allowing recall and the invocation of relationships. This communication model allows you to say something without actually saying it. It can be indispensable when you are trying to communicate covertly. Negotiation

Contrary to popular belief, most negotiations, even for a business leader, happen outside the boardroom. Any time you try to make someone with a different view come across to thinking like you and doing what you want is a time you are negotiating. With that being said, you will do a lot more negotiating in your new position as a manager. The stakes will also be higher, so it is something you might want to perfect.

Building your negotiation skills

NLP teaches about outcome setting using fundamental approaches. With an outcome setting, you learn how to win in a negotiation by recognizing a few important facts about negotiation. These include:

Information is key to negotiation

Negotiation is a form of decision making. In fact, the decisions you make during and at the end of negotiation are the most important ones you will ever make. When you are more informed, you negotiate better and make healthier decisions. To do this, you might have to get the professional services of an investment consultant, a headhunter, a lawyer, or an accountant. These professionals clarify some of the more complicated things for you and also give advice. With sufficient information, you will be better placed to understand the whole scope of the situation and also to reach a winning deal.

Moreover, information flows faster in a negotiation than any other time. The situation you leave in a morning negotiation could be very different from the one you find in the afternoon. If you buy a software package shortly before a more superior one enters the market, it will leave your company at a huge disadvantage when all your rivals adopt better technology and start to outperform you. A slight change creates a massive shift, and anyone who doesn't know or appreciate the changes risks getting screwed over in the negotiation. Keep your finger on the pulse, as the saying goes, to avoid possible ramifications down the line.

Anything is only as valuable as the buyer makes it

People set the value of objects based on the value they perceive it has, not necessarily its real value. For example, hardly anyone ever complains about the cost of healthcare because people value their health more. The same rule applies to negotiations. Whatever is under contention will be valued based on the perception of the marginal buyer, i.e., the person who is interested in it. You can sell something for more than its market share if you can capitalize on the interest another person shows in it.

You are not immune from influence

Sometimes, we make the decision to do something based on impulse rather than good reason. Skilled negotiators use psychological principles like reciprocation, social proof, and scarcity to influence their rivals into giving ground beyond the make-sense point. Let's touch briefly on these principles.

Reciprocation exploits the evolutionary urge every human being has to reward every good deed with another. So, rather than start with exactly what you came to the negotiation table for, a wily negotiator will give their rival a "free" gift, often out of the blue. Even though we may not be aware of it or we fight hard against it when we are aware, studies have shown that we are more likely to concede ground when we feel that we are reciprocating.

Social proof is a tool whose use many salespeople have perfected to an art form. You go to buy something, say conferencing equipment for your office, with a pretty concrete idea of the qualities you want in mind. It is cheap, reliable, and recommended. But the salesperson you meet, working for a different company selling a different product, convinces you to buy something more expensive simply because they tell you that it is the equipment that Mark Cuban or Zuckerberg uses. Your desire to fit in leaves you susceptible to manipulation.

Finally, we have the oldest but still most effective trick in the book—scarcity. People value scarce things higher and will be willing to pay more for something simply because the opportunity is closing or there is a short supply. The worst mistakes made on the negotiation table are those that followed one party (often the most unlikely) pulling out or expressing the desire to pull out.

How to make it a win-win

The outcome of a negotiation defines the relationship you will have with your negotiating rival afterward. If you crush someone in a negotiation, he or she will probably be left feeling cheated and taken advantage of. This tends to happen when you go to the negotiation with a must-win mentality—the notion that the other person must lose for you to be satisfied. Any concession you give to your rival will make you feel cheated, which results in mutual dissatisfaction on both sides. So, the disaster of approaching a negotiation with a must-win mentality is not just that you destroy any chance at a relationship afterward but that it also turns out to be a lose-lose outcome.

A much better approach, especially in the long run, is to find a way for both of you to walk out of the negotiation with what you wanted. If that is not possible (and that is the case most of the time), then at least you should both come out feeling satisfied with the outcome. This is where it gets a little complicated and where NLP comes in handy.

By using the NLP strategy of total-win, you foster cooperation, rather than competition, with your negotiation rival by using strategies such as:

Establish your positions

Three out of five times when people reach a stalemate in a negotiation, it is because they are too fixated on getting their own way or they misunderstand what the other party wants.

Nevertheless, people will go out of their way to try and make sure that their adversary doesn't get the thing they think he or she wants. Keeping an open mind is important when you are going into a negotiation. Make no assumptions about your rival's interests. In fact, you should be as clear as possible as to what they hope to gain from the negotiation.

When Steve Jobs was buying the parts to build his first computer, he negotiated two deals with two different merchants, one to get the parts he needed to build the computer and the other to market the computer—on credit. Without this genius piece of negotiation, the Macintosh may never have been born.

What are the interests?

Whatever your position in a negotiation, your interest in the outcome will always be infinitely bigger. You try to negotiate with the best salesman in your field because you want to bring him to your team—that is your position. But what you really want is to become the best-performing junior manager in your company—that is your interest. See, it is very easy to negotiate for our own interests because they are the very thing that drives us.

Understanding the other person's interests, however, can be a little bit more complicated. It requires a level of empathy and consideration that many of us don't have. But if you can discover your rival's interests, you will have gained the key to winning the negotiation for both of you. Interests can be driven by everything from tangible gains to beliefs, cultural values, and status. And because people rarely ever do anything that is against their values, it is something you need to appreciate during a negotiation.

Focus on achieving mutual gain

Good leaders know exactly what to do to get their way. Great leaders try to make sure that everyone gets a good deal out of their dealings with them. This calls for the ability to brainstorm as many inventive ideas to reach an agreement as will be needed to find the one solution that enriches both teams. Even when you crush an opponent in a negotiation, you can reframe the outcome so that they don't feel like they lost too much.

The conditional close is one way that mutual gain can be implied even when it is not, in the strictest terms, achieved. The conditional close is used to overcome objections with the promise of a sentimental reward that your partner did not expect but may value more. This requires that you understand their interests so that you can twist arguments around to appeal to them. The conditional close could be anything from promising to give a reluctant target hireling an indoor mini-golf course if they sign a five-year deal to promising to buy all your supplies from one seller if they give you a really big discount. The conditional close momentarily removes the negotiation from the key issues and boosts your chances of winning. It can be especially effective when your interest in the outcome of a negotiation is outsized and your chances of winning are low.

Compromise

In every negotiation, an agreement can only be achieved by the willingness of both parties to settle. This is called compromising, whereby each one of you gives something up to get closer to the other person's position. The best compromise is one that is created from the objective analysis of your own position. Before starting the negotiation process, sit down and ask yourself what you are willing to give up. Be objective about it but keep it under wraps until you get down to ironing out a settlement. Ideally, you should convince your rival to take your position without giving anything up. But when it comes down to it, it is much better when you know exactly what you can and cannot give up.

The BATNA, or Best Alternative to a Negotiated Agreement, is a kind of alternative outcome every party in a negotiation has. If you negotiate with the best salesman in the city to join your team but realize that he or she is too costly an acquisition, your BATNA might be to get the second-best or incentivize your own team. A good BATNA helps you go through negotiation without falling for a terrible deal simply because you think there is no option.

Influencing others

As much as you will try to make a negotiation ends with a win-win situation, you must cultivate the ability to influence others. Look at it this way; it is better to hold all the cards and be generous than count on the generosity of other people to get what you want. As a leader, you want to leave nothing to chance. You want to have the power to influence the outcome of negotiation as much as possible. Well, with NLP techniques like rapport, mirroring, and pattern interruption, you can get just that.

Building Rapport

The ability to reach a satisfactory win-win settlement in a negotiation relies in part on your ability to establish a connection with your negotiation partner. In the last chapter, we touched on rapport as part of the Milton model of communication. Well, turns out making eye contact, synchronizing body language, and matching vocal patterns also help you in negotiation. This helps you reduce the chances of cognitive dissonance and puts your partner more at ease. All round, rapport building creates a connection that makes it easier to come to a favorable conclusion.

Pattern interruption

Pattern interruption is a very powerful, subtle mind-control tool. When you make someone do a series of actions a few times, their unconscious mind takes over and starts to expect the next action in the series. This establishes a pattern. Breaking the pattern entails simply removing one of the actions in the series and redirecting the person into doing something they normally wouldn't have done. Some mentalists use pattern interruption to achieve results as impressive as talking strangers into giving them their wallets. You can employ pattern interruption along with other NLP techniques like anchoring and metaphors to establish a quid pro quo of actions that results in you getting what you want.

NLP negotiation exercise

One of the most effective NLP negotiation exercises is the agreement frame. It follows a simple procedure of pacing and leading to influence the pace, direction, and outcome of a negotiation. The steps are:

1. You open the negotiation by telling the other party your expectations and the solution you want.

2. Ask your partner to state their best offer for what you want

3. Use pacing and directing to agree AND offer a counterproposal. Avoid words like but, however, and other such contradictory terms.

4. Work towards a greater agreement by discussing your positions and the interests behind them. It is always best when you get the other party talking about their interests in making the deal because it gives you clues as to what conditions you

can give for a mutually beneficial close.

5. Talk to the other party into agreeing with your condition by highlighting the benefits and downplaying any perceived weaknesses.

6. Check that there are no objections and close the negotiation as swiftly as possible.

Presentation

Public speaking is an important skill for a business leader to have. Good presentation skills allow you to talk to a large group of people and pass on the information you need to. Presentations serve the purpose of informing, demonstrating, persuading, and inspiring. They make up a big part of leadership communication.

Over the course of your career, you will be requested to make presentations to present detailed information to your employees, seniors, and or peers. Demonstrational presentations are useful for showing how a product works. It can be for a new technology you are hoping to adopt or the prototype of a new product for your company to produce. Persuasive presentations are more important because they are supposed to appeal to the audience and generate a specific reaction (agreement) from them that they might not be very willing to give. Finally, the ability to make inspirational presentations can come in handy when you need to motivate and stir up the interest of your employees and peers towards a specific course of action. For example, the presentation you make while selling your vision for the department is inspirational.

You can make the same kind of convincing and inspirational speeches that Steve Jobs used to sell his iPhone. But to do this you need to use NLP techniques. They entail:

Two-minute anecdotes

An anecdote gives you the perfect start to the speech. It can be a story about something that happened to you, an interesting article you recently read, or a statistic. If you make it humorous, an anecdote will also break the ice and leave you feeling more confident about talking to your audience. Steve Jobs opened up his presentations with a thought-provoking story that got the audience hooked on his every word.

He also used one-word notes for his presentations that made it easier for the audience to recall what he said.

Use sensory language

Words can be used to invoke all five sensory experiences of sound, sight, feel, taste, and smell. The use of these words pulls the audience into the plane of thought you have created and allows you to appeal directly to their senses. Steve Jobs was able to peg his audience to his every word by using carefully worded statements that turned ordinarily boring and technical presentations into engaging and awe-inspiring ones.

Anchoring

A good presenter uses the stage in a very particular way. Instead of just moving around, designate specific areas of the stage for specific types of information to unconsciously engage the audience in the presentation. For example, if you choose to be tough in the center-forward position, firm on the left, and playful on the right, your audience will unconsciously expect to feel these reactions whenever you get to those positions.

Anchoring can also be accomplished using gestures. If you watch Steve Jobs's presentation, you will notice that he does it quite a lot. Animated gestures (in moderation) engage the visual sensors and draw attention to your nonverbal cues while on stage. The nonverbal cues, in turn, allow the audience to absorb all of the information that comes from your mouth.

Focus on the aim, not the content

The outcome of a speech is more important than the content of the speech itself. Focusing on the ways your speech will affect the audience rather than the things you will say helps you develop your presentation skills in a number of ways.

1. You are more intentional in the words you use.

2. It imparts the need for you to work harder to connect to the audience.

3. Taking the focus from what you will say reduces the anxiety of making a presentation.

For Jobs, it was usually to drum up support for a new product, and people would line up outside Apple stores to buy his product. He would sell the benefits with simple yet effective visuals. Because he understood that the aim of communicating is to elicit a specific feeling, Steve Jobs perfected the art of presentation in his years at Apple. Today, he is one of the most admired and studied business leaders in history. The biggest attraction point, especially for managers, is his presentations.

Chapter 6: Anxiety and stress management

Anxiety and stress are quite common in the demanding life of a leader. They are two commonly related issues but are caused by quite different mental and physical states. You will feel stressed when the demands of your workplace or new changes put a strain on your mental and physical faculties. Anxiety, on the other hand, comes about when you dread or are worried about a future situation. The main difference between anxiety and stress is that the former mostly occurs before a demanding event while the latter commonly follows afterward. In this chapter, we will look at the two states and how they can affect your ability to perform as a newly promoted manager.

Anxiety

Anxiety occurs when we feel threatened by external factors or, surprisingly, when we are anxious. It adds "freeze" to "fight or flight" and makes it harder for you to do things that other people find easy. Unlike stress, anxiety is a mental condition that can impair social and professional functioning in the long term. And even when anxiety occurs for a short span, the impact can be just as serious to your social and professional life.

Causes of anxiety

Some of the reasons why you might be feeling anxious include:

Self-doubt

Normally, people use to fight or fight to tackle big problems, either fighting it out or fleeing to avoid dealing with them. But when you are about to embark on a huge inevitable task but you don't feel capable, you are trapped in what your mind perceives to be an impossible situation. You cannot run and you feel incapable of fighting, so your mind settles for option three and freezes up. This form of anxiety is very common when you are faced with a huge task.

Limiting thoughts contribute to self-doubt by making you feel incapable of doing something. Whether from previous experiences or lack of previous experiences, your brain can make you feel fearful (of going back to a place where you have failed before) or worried (about the prospect of doing something you have never done before) and cause you lots of anxiety.

Choices

For people who are prone to anxiety, the choice can be very incapacitating. It paves the way for self-doubts about your ability to make the right one. Big choices with serious consequences are especially notorious for inducing stress. Making a choice under pressure, where the chances of making a mistake are even higher, is even more anxiety-inducing. People who are prone to anxiety tend to find the process of making a decision daunting, spending hours worrying about the chance of making a mistake. The choice mostly causes anxiety among those with anxiety disorders rather than common bouts of anxiety. The anxiety caused by choice points to a lack of confidence in making decisions.

For leaders, choosing between two bad options with bad results means that people might lose their livelihood, careers might be destroyed, or other bad consequences might follow. Even with great decision-making capabilities, the choice could still cause anxiety.

Lack of options

On the other hand, the lack of choice is just as anxiety-inducing. The choice is a reason why freedom is one of the most important things for humans and why democracy is celebrated as the best form of government worldwide. On a personal level, nothing makes people as anxious as the perception that they are trapped in a bad situation. When you have to choose between two choices that will both lead to adversity, the very idea of having to deal with any of the consequences could freeze you right up. A sensation of entrapment often results and anxious feelings crop up.

Preventing anxiety

To ensure that anxiety does not interfere with your work, you must use NLP to avoid it. If you can manage to overcome anxiety before it happens, you will live a happy, fulfilled life. Your ability to lead will also improve dramatically. Some of the strategies you can use to get there include:

Rename it

The things that scare us are often daunting in name only. When you actually think about them, they are actually quite harmless. The idea of renaming the things that cause you to be anxious borrows from the NLP technique of reframing. Simply put a positive spin on things: challenges are growth opportunities, the opposition is a chance to win big, and failure is just a minor setback. By reframing, you also put things in perspective so that you don't have to beat yourself up or be apprehensive about future events that are not even in your control.

Limit your choices

If the idea of making a choice makes you anxious, then you must find a way to make choices in advance. A clearly stated vision is the first place to start. It narrows down your options to only those things that help you move closer to the ultimate goal. Making your choices through visionary thinking further enhances your decision-making capabilities and reduces the level of your anxiety overall.

In the rare event that you have no option but to decide between two or more options, a pros-and-cons list can be a simple yet elegantly effective tool. It narrows your choices and gives you a way to make choices in an objective manner.

Create an exit strategy

The reason why most people feel trapped in the notion that they have no option whatsoever. To avoid the possibility of that ever happening, an exit strategy or plan B comes in handy. Even as you dedicate all your energies to achieve plan A, the knowledge that you have a backup plan in case anything goes wrong is both reassuring and settling. An exit strategy is especially important if you are prone to anxiety attacks.

NLP treatment

In the event that anxiety gets past your defense systems (and this is highly likely), you can use still use the following NLP strategies to remedy it.

Change your thinking about anxiety
Anxiety hinders so many people from achieving their goals because it comes as a double threat. The real instance of anxiety happens when the dread of doing something causes you to freeze and be unable to do it. But sometimes the anxiety happens much earlier, when you start fearing the freeze before it actually happens— anxiety about anxiety. This is because most people who have experienced negative impacts of anxiety—missed deadlines, failed tasks, and poor performance—start to associate their failures with the anxiety attacks. It becomes a big threat to their wellbeing and easily gets blown out of proportion.

NLP anxiety training helps you overcome it by helping you recognize that anxiety is actually nothing. It is simply a creation out of your own mind, a monster of your own making that nevertheless terrorizes you. Anxiety is not even an emotion; it is a thought process that happens when you face a threatening situation. When you change the way you think about anxiety, you will start to normalize it and, at the very least, tackle any anxiety you might have about anxiety, which only makes it worse.

Turn it around

You can use the NLP presupposition of the capacity to turn your thinking about anxiety around. The NLP presupposition of capacity states that we are only incapacitated by our own minds. Realize that what is in the future cannot hurt you now unless you represent it to yourself as something that can hurt you. When you worry endlessly about something, you only increase the creation of double jeopardy whereby you will suffer for an event that might not even happen and because it has already happened in your mind, the chances of it happening in the real world also increase.

So, if you are anxious because you think a huge deal you have been negotiating for your company might fall apart and get you fired, you will be unable to focus on getting it done, fail, and get fired anyway. But if you turn an anxiety-causing event around and make it less of a big deal, your own fears about it will diminish as well.

Be in the moment
What anxiety does that is so devastating is that it deceives our minds into believing that our worst fears are real and happening at the moment. So, not only does it rob us of the opportunity to live every moment of our life, it transports us into the worst-case scenario future. But you can overcome it by remaining rooted in the present moment, doing what you can do to make the future as beautiful as possible. You can use self-hypnosis to remove the negative images of the future from your mind, swatting them away any time they try to resurface. Experience every moment of your day and only consider the future in an objective manner.

Know what you can and cannot do
We are most anxious about the things we think we are supposed to be able to do even when they are completely impossible. You will never be anxious about crashing a spacecraft into Mars because you know that would never happen.

Only the things that you are capable of doing will make you anxious. The limit of your anxiety, therefore, is the limit of your potential.

Do it anyway

Nelson Mandela said, "It always seems impossible until it is done." This is true for every task that makes you anxious. As difficult as it seems, at one point you will look at it and remember a time when you thought you couldn't do it. Splitting up a huge job into smaller tasks can make you feel more confident about your ability to do it. Once you have started to do it, you will start to feel less scared of doing it and effectively banish your anxiety. The trick is to not be afraid to feel the fear because fear is part of the achievement.

Harnessing anxiety to excel

Studies have shown that brain anxiety can unlock certain parts of the brain and enable you to do so much. People with high levels of anxiety can use their panic and worry to function at a more productive level. This can be done by following the following process:

Allowing anxiety

The first and most important process in harnessing anxiety is to accept that you are anxious. But instead of thinking of your anxiety as being destructive, think of it as a force of nature that sharpens your reflexes, heightens your awareness, and gives you greater strength. This takes the fear away from the equation and allows you to go to the next step in the process.

Befriend your anxiety

Think of your anxiety as a wild stallion. You cannot tame it if you don't calm it down enough to ride it. Understand the causes of your anxiety so that you can get into the right position to solve them. Instead of thinking of it as the enemy, think of it as the sentry alerting you to a problem. The sensations you feel are simply your body trying to get you ready for some action. Let the anxiety fill you at your terms. Feel it increasing sensation to your arms, legs, and mind. Feel the adrenaline pumping through your system, giving you strength, focus, stamina, and speed. There's nothing to worry about here!

Channel it

As the energy, stamina, focus, and speed course through your body bring your mind about to the thing you've got to do. Focus the anxiety towards the activity at hand and visualize yourself getting into the state of flow. Anxiety will be your fuel until you emerge, having accomplished the task you set out to do. If you can create a productive relationship with your anxiety, there is no reason why you shouldn't be able to achieve new levels of success and productivity in your new career.

Stress

Stress occurs in less subtle ways than anxiety, and prolonged stress is actually believed to be the leading cause of a majority of lifestyle diseases because it affects the functioning of organs, worsens the effects of cancer, and hampers circulation. The thing about stress is that unlike anxiety, it is very real and very often completely warranted.

Causes of stress

In your management career, stress can come from many areas. A bad working relationship with a senior manager can be a stressful thing because he or she can make your work so much harder. Constant failure in your pursuit of a vision or a goal can also be very stressful.

Lack of work-life balance

As you settle down into your new job, you will almost certainly have to apply yourself even harder to the job. Sometimes, this means that your home life suffers. A bad work-life balance can be extremely stressful because it means that you will have no conduit to drain the stress of your job at the end of the day.

Poor health

Your new job comes with added responsibilities that with most likely turn your life upside down. Your old healthy habits fall off and your eating habits deteriorate. This all leads to decreased energy levels, energy drinks and coffee, poor sleeping habits, and increased levels of stress.

Poor planning

"Failing to plan is planning to fail" so the saying goes. Well, turns out that poor planning is also a recipe for stress. Poor planning means that you never foresee challenges and put in place the measures to mitigate them. You will face numerous problems that make it harder to achieve your intended outcome, increase the pressure of your job, and blow up your stress levels.

Stress management

Slow down

Sometimes all the body needs are the opportunity to recharge. When you don't give yourself some downtime to replenish your energies, you only increase your stress levels. Even when you are engaged in a big project, taking a break can be very crucial in alleviating your stress levels. Go out for a drink, watch a movie, sit and read a book, just take your mind off whatever is giving you stress.

If you simply cannot find the time to slow down, you can use NLP's future pacing to achieve the same effect for a fraction of the time.

1. Simply recall a time when you were calm, relaxed, and at peace.

2. Close your eyes and focus on that one thought

3. Expand the details and immerse yourself fully into the picture. Activate all the sensory organs for a more realistic experience.

When your mind relaxes, so does your body. All the stressors will be dispelled, and you will be left feeling refreshed and more alert.

Create awareness

As much as people maintain that their stress is caused by a bad boss, difficult project, or whatever they attribute their stress to, nothing ever stresses you out without you giving it the permission to do so. The way you react to a situation is the real culprit. If you deliberately choose to not get stressed, then that will be your new reality. Whenever you feel a negative reaction to a distressing event building up, practice the following NLP exercise:

1. Take 10 deep breaths

2. Bring your mind to the present and be wide aware of everything about you. Activate every sense to perceive the current situation as clearly as possible

3. Visualize a present moment when everything is perfect, and you have no reason whatsoever to worry

4. Realize that you really don't have to be worried about a thing

Be positive

The best weapon to deal with stress is to be positive on purpose. When you let your brain process thoughts at its usual rate, 70% of what goes through your mind will always be negative. It is only when you are mindfully positive that you can be positive indeed and overcome stress. Whenever a negative thought comes to mind, accept it as one among many and replace it with the direct opposite (positive thought). Think about your goals, past happy times, and anything that makes you feel excited and you will achieve a state of true optimism and positivity and stop the stress even before it happens.

Make time for family and to hang out with friends

Work-life balance is critical to stress avoidance. Keeping in touch with your support group offers a great source for stress relief and positivity.

Have a laugh

If you have to watch cat videos or watch stand-up comedy to laugh, do it. A good laugh is one of the best tonics for stress. The more you do it, the less stress you will have to deal with.

NLP stress management

Any one of the following NLP exercises can be very effective for stress management;

1. Simply floating your awareness out of the body can help you to disconnect from a stressful situation into an imagined world of peace and tranquility.

2. Imagine that there is a glass wall in front of you and all the things that are stressing you are on the other side. They cannot get to you because you are protected by the glass shield

3. Turn down the volume of the stressful thoughts going through your mind until they are quiet. This includes any negative self-talk associated with a stressful event

4. Send the images away, away, away. Stress sometimes manifests as ugly images going through our minds. To remove the stress, imagine the images leaving your mind and propel them as far away from you as possible.

Chapter 7: Motivation

We pursue goals and visions because we are motivated to do so. As a leader, you will need to stay driven and focused on the vision for your department. The job of keeping your employees hungry for more achievements will also fall on you. Your ability to keep everyone motivated will affect your productivity and, ultimately, your success. In this chapter, we will look at how you can use NLP to keep both yourself and your employees motivated even in the face of failure.

NLP techniques to motivate yourself

The following strategies have been used by the majority of the world's most successful business leaders to get where they are today. I hope that using them will make you stay motivated and driven to excel more today than you did yesterday.

Focus on one thing

The first tip for motivation is focusing on one thing at a time. This might be harder when you are a manager and your to-do list is overflowing with tasks, but trying to do more than one thing at one time will only lead to overloading yourself, probable failure, and disenchantment.

Motivation comes, in most part, from the confidence you gain over time because you can do something really well. In fact, it is very hard to remain motivated after failure. This is why businessmen like Elon Musk, who has continued with the same passion even after failure, are so inspirational.

Discover your big WHY

The reason why Elon Musk, Steve Jobs, Tony Robbins, Bill Gates, and any other successful leader have all continued pursuing excellence to the top of their fields was that they were doing something that gave their lives purpose. Each one of us has that one thing, but most are not even aware of what it is. But if you want to stay motivated, if you want to surprise yourself with superhuman feats of drive and ambition, find the one thing that will give your life meaning. What you are doing matters little if the reason why you are doing it does not align with your life purpose. And when you do something because it aligns with your big WHY, you can withstand any challenges and remain strong enough to pursue it regardless of your failures.

You should apply the big why on a project-by-project basis. Any good manager has a clear-cut vision that drives their every action. Whenever you do something, answer the question of why the desired outcome will contribute to the fulfillment of your dream. You will realize that your motivation in doing something will be as compelling as the reason why you are doing it.

Visualize your goal

Visualization is a powerful motivational tool. It connects your body, your mind, and your emotions and works as the fuel that powers your motivation to work. To help your mind along, create a specific representation of your goal as possible. Use all the senses to visualize the moment of success, and if possible, a visual representation. When you visualize a specific, rather than vague outcome, your emotions and your body take over and start to help you to get there.

Picture the worst

As we discussed in chapter 6 above, our brain has the capacity to expand and accomplish exceptional feats. Untrained, this expansion of the mind pours over as anxiety. But when we tame this beast, we can harness the power of the anxious mind for motivation. You see, our brains respond exceptionally well to a negative stimulus versus positive. So, while visualization is a valid tool for the attainment of goals, picturing not achieving an outcome is even more terrifying and easier for the brain to do.

If you can see the outcome of not achieving your goal on the second, third, and nth try, chances are that your brain will already be terrified by the third level of consequences. This serves as the perfect deterrent to your mind, which will then lead to you doing anything you can to make sure that it does not happen. This serves as the "away from" motivation, what you are trying to avoid by working hard.

Picture the benefits

More than just picturing yourself achieving your goal, there are numerous benefits to be reaped from imagining the perfect world of achievement after reaching your goal. It works as an additional "toward" image to your visualization, albeit in a wider and less intense way. Picturing simply entails daydreams of the consequences of achieving a goal.

Your employee lifting your shoulder higher, popping champagne, an article about your genius in *The Wall Street Journal*. It is all very invigorating to think about it. And the best thing is that even though you will be motivated by the visions, it is highly unlikely that you will be disappointed when they don't happen because you will already be pretty damn thrilled to have reached the goal!

Don't overreach

It is all right to dream and have a big vision, but you must make sure that your dream/vision is within the make-sense zone. Things that are beyond your control only serve as a recipe for disaster because you will hardly ever achieve them. The only outcome worth pursuing is one that is within your control to get. When the goal is unrealistic, our brains often respond by shutting up, creating even more anxiety and making it harder to find the motivation to work.

Know the price

For everything you commit to pursuing, you will be foregoing putting your focus on something else of equal or more value. Family, relationships, and other interests are some of the things that you might have to give up (or have less of) to achieve your biggest goal. You should only commit to doing something after figuring out the price you will have to pay for it and determining that you are okay with it.

Measure your progress

When you set a vision to work towards, make it measurable. The work involved in subdividing it into smaller tasks and budgeting for time and other resources will also help you determine whether or not it is achievable. You can then measure your progress along the way to verify that you are on track as well as for motivation. See, what you will find out is that even the smallest evidence of progress can be very motivational. When you are feeling overwhelmed, looking at the progress you have made over time can push you to work even harder to get to your destination.

Make a total commitment

One of the leading causes of procrastination is future options: the notion that something will happen in the future to make your life that much better. The reason why this causes people to procrastinate is that it kills the motivation to work right now. Few people would work now if they were assured of being all set in the future. The mind is no different. It shuts up and ceases functioning (at least in part) when there is an opening for that.

Failing to commit 100% to a decision only makes room for doubts, lethargy, and laziness. As soon as you make up your mind to pursue a certain outcome, you should banish every other option from your mind. Even a plan B, while essential, can be an excuse for your mind to half-ass its way through plan A.

Create the right environment

Your environment plays a big role in the pursuit of any outcome you set out to achieve. Environmental obstacles can either be physical or mental. Both can be detrimental to motivation. Environmental obstacles can be avoided by changing locations or refurnishing your office if your furniture is blocking your motivation. You must be willing to do what you need to do to get your mind in the right state for productivity. Mental obstacles are somewhat more serious killers of motivation because they are a bit harder to banish. If you want to achieve a particular goal, you must get your mind in the right state; otherwise, you won't find the incentive to do much.

Get the right people

The only way to grow your motivation is to insert yourself in a nurturing environment. This means that you must surround yourself with positive, growth-minded people who will add to your energies rather than draining them. The good thing is that as the manager, you have almost free reign to hire the right people. A good team will not just tolerate you; they will support your dream for the department heartily and with good cheer.

We will discuss motivating your team below, but this is also a contributing factor to your own motivation and must be mentioned here. Your ability to follow the guidelines discussed below to create a motivated team will have a cyclic impact on your own motivation.

Start working in advance

Chance favors the prepared, so the saying goes. Well, so does motivation. The best way to keep yourself motivated all day long is to have a clear idea of what you will be doing in the day. So, obviously, the best time to plan for your day's activity is yesterday.

And before going to sleep, it is good to take a few minutes to look through the to-do list for the next day. Look over the items on that list and visualize, very briefly, yourself doing them. Don't go into the details. Just make sure that it is the last thing that you think of before falling asleep. Your mind will be working on the items subconsciously through the night so that you will wake up feeling energized and eager to start working. This also helps you say no to distractions.

Use the Pareto principle

The Pareto equation states that 80% of your outcomes will be generated by 20% of your efforts. The most effective people are skilled at determining the 20% and focusing their energies on it. They are able to achieve more with less effort and retain much of their energy, being always motivated and ready to rock it out. When you are a leader, your job should be to figure out ways of achieving the best results with limited resources. The Pareto principle can be a great way to ensure that your resource allocation produces the most outcomes. It is also very gratifying on a personal level when you see such massive results as 80% from doing 20% of something. It grows your motivation exponentially.

Focus

You have probably heard about the exceptional power of NO. As a manager, you should learn to say no to shallow work like logistical support that does not require any special skills. Instead, focus on the deep work, taking the lead on the accomplishment of mentally demanding jobs that will allow you to get into that state of flow where motivation and skills meet to produce exceptional levels of productivity.

In the current content-filled world, take pride in being delightfully ignorant of memes, comfortably absent from "hot" social media trends, and hard to reach. Unless you are a social media manager, these distractions do nothing to make you better at your work.

Fake it till you make it

Now I know that this is a contentious concept, but it is also one of the most effective tools for personal motivation. Regardless of what people say, the people who act as if they are already achievers in whatever field their desires lie are infinitely more motivated than the rest of us. They have achieved something that few others can ever boast of having—a state of perpetual visualization. Furthermore, isn't modeling a critical concept of NLP? If you decide to start acting as you have already reached the levels you want to get to, your brain reacts by thinking like the image you have made for yourself. Acting as if you have already reached your outcome motivates you to work the hardest to make it a reality.

NLP techniques to motivate others

Motivating others is a skill that every manager needs because it falls on him or her to motivate his entire staff. The best leaders are able to motivate their teams to achieve above and beyond everyone's expectations. You can motivate your team by using the strategies of coaching, relationships, dialogue, and credibility.

Coaching

Motivation in the workplace comes from the confidence of being able to do one's work competently. This is especially critical for the employees who perform the technical jobs in the company. And since motivation goes hand in hand with the ability to do their job well, increasing their competence is guaranteed to boost your employees' impetus to work.

As a manager, you will be responsible for molding your junior employees in accordance with your vision for your division. The mentoring you do encourages them to pursue excellence, increases their skill set, and motivates them, all at the same time. You can even go a step further and hire professionals to teach curricular and extracurricular skills. The more the skills your employees have, the greater the dedication they will show to their job.

Relationships

The environment you create for your employees will play a big role in their dedication to working. It is important that you foster a relationship with every member of the team. Find out their interests and talents and figure out the best way to match them with the company objectives. That way, every member of your team will have a role to play in the pursuit of your vision and you can all draw motivation from each other.

The relationships you create with your employees form a two-way support system which will come in handy when you are dealing with stress. A support system of coworkers is more effective in the management of stress because you all have a firsthand understanding of the stressful conditions you face. A nurturing environment boosts morale and motivates every member of your team to work even harder.

Team building

Team-building exercises do a lot to foster relationships. Whether you will take your whole team to full-day or weekend getaways or you will keep the bonding at the workplace, conducting NLP exercises like visualization can create a very strong bond between employees and contribute towards a nurturing environment where every employee is motivated to achieve the best.

Rapport is a very important thing to foster a team spirit. So, ensure that you use the smallest excuse for teamwork to make your team do the same thing, even aerobic exercises. It connects everyone together and, when you are at the forefront of the rapport-building activity, cements your position as the leader. And because of the rapport you have established with them, your team will be more likely to keep an open mind when considering and implementing your ideas.

Dialogues

With every word to speak, you have the opportunity to motivate someone or crush their spirit. This is especially true when you are in a position of influence because your opinion is highly regarded. So, whenever you speak to your employees, you must watch your words to avoid killing their motivation. Even criticism should be offered in a constructive manner or not offered at all. But constructive criticism is not the only way to motivate others through communication. You can also use vision setting and presentations for this.

Vision

The vision acts like a stimulus that channels the relationships and allows a large team to cooperate in the attainment of a common goal. Using an NLP principle called the logical levels of change, you take the company blueprint and apply it to the six levels of thinking. At the workplace, you start with the environment and surround your whole team with the concepts of your vision and mission. This serves as their own personal vision and mission whenever they are at work and motivates the highest levels of productivity.

Speeches and presentations

Another way to motivate others is to make speeches or presentations. This is a strategy that has been used by some of the world's greatest leaders. In the early days of Microsoft, Bill Gates used to make his entrance to the company's annual general meeting in dramatic fashion, including an incident when he rode in with a gang of Harley Davidson bikers. He and his cofounder would then rouse their employees with song, dance, and drink to celebrate every financial year of great results. The motivation and productivity of his employees remained at all-time high levels all through the 70s and 80s and enabled him to get closer to his vision of putting Microsoft software on every computer in the world.

Other leaders who use charismatic motivational tools to energize and motivate employees are the duo of Warren Buffett and Charlie Munger. To this day, these two celebrated leaders hold an annual general meeting where presentations usually include humorous videos of the two men. The Berkshire Hathaway AGM is one of the most popular events in the city of Omaha where it is held.

Credibility

As much as the vision is supposed to have the input of everyone in your team, it is essentially your prerogative to think about the future of the department by considering the overall vision of the company and how your department can contribute towards it. People follow leaders they can trust, and teams that have no clear leader always fall apart because there is no direction. So, to make sure that the team pursues your vision with gusto, ensure that you exhibit the qualities of integrity, intent, capability, and results.

Integrity means that you don't apply double standards when dealing with your employees. Don't treat anyone better or act in an entitled manner. The hardest working person should always be you.

People trust men and women who show good intentions for everything they do. Even if someone does not agree with something you did, they will judge you less harshly if your motivations were not ill meant.

It matters a lot whether you got to your current position by merit. People respect capable leaders, and your capability and skill set should be impeccable to earn the respect of your team. Incidentally, people with high capabilities value capability in a leader even higher. Therefore, this is a quality you will want to cultivate if you want to get to the levels of productivity you desire.

In the end, little else matters apart from the results. If you constantly achieve beyond their wildest imagination, people will hold you in high regard and be more willing to do what you ask of them.

Conclusion

Neuro-linguistic programming (NLP) is the art and science of using mental models and language to alter harmful behaviors we exhibit into constructive ones. There are numerous techniques of NLP, but some are, naturally, more applicable than others. Future pacing is one of the most powerful and easily applicable NLP techniques. It allows us to visualize desired outcomes to get motivated to work and also helps us shift our perceptions of the present to overcome anxiety and stress. The swish pattern is another indispensable NLP technique that helps us to modify behavior by replacing negative thoughts with positive ones. It is very important to behavior change. In hypnosis and persuasion, metaphors come in very handy. By simply implanting an idea into the mind of a target, you can recruit their subconscious mind to work in your favor to convince someone to do whatever you want. Reframing allows us to adopt a new perspective to a situation, focusing on the positive rather than negative for perpetual positivity. Finally, anchoring helps us create associations between events and our minds by employing gestures and words as memory anchors. This makes it easier to recall a memory and comes in handy for stress reduction and improved self-confidence.

You must have noticed that vision was mentioned is almost every chapter of the book as a factor affecting everything from problem-solving, decision making, time management, stress management, and pretty much everything you do as a leader. Your vision powers everything you do as a leader. You will only be as successful as you let yourself be and you will do this with a vision too big, too small, or SMART. This condition applies to personal and team success. If you can manage to sell your vision for the division you lead and get the team to buy into the idea enough to fully commit, you will most probably achieve massive success. And most of the NLP techniques discussed throughout this book have something to do with vision setting or achievement. They include anchoring, future pacing, well-formed outcome, and state management. Even reframing, swish, and covert hypnosis that help modify behavior contribute to our pursuit of the vision by putting us in the right frame of mind.

Thinking is a big part of what you will be doing as a manager, so it is very important that you do it right. We discussed the ways you can apply

NLP techniques to your thinking, problem-solving, and decision making. This will be immensely critical to your career. Because the one thing that sets apart the world's best leaders like Elon Musk, Warren Buffett, and Steve Jobs, among others, is their unique thinking. They applied their unique thinking styles to innovate and to solve problems as they arose. They were defined by the big decisions they made, and so will you. We also offered some NLP exercises to help you to start thinking like a leader and win like the best business leaders who ever lived. Only when you have mastered these techniques will you be in a position to step into your destiny and achieve the vision you have crafted not just for you, but for your whole team.

Results make leaders. We also touched on the importance of productivity for your career, including the NLP techniques and exercises that you can use to attain the highest levels of productivity. The most important tip for efficiency—understanding the way the brain works and tailoring your work around the high peaks of productivity. And to find the state of flow with your whole team, we described a series of NLP exercises that include anchoring your wins and visualizing the goal of every task you embark on.

With its close relation to linguistics, communication turned out to be an important message in the book. It plays a big part in sharing your goal, negotiating successfully, and motivating your employees. With NLP, you can unlock unconscious messaging, an element of communication that most people overlook. With unconscious communication, your negotiation and presentations (both critical to good leadership) will be boosted. You can then use negotiations to foster good relations with partners by ensuring that everyone wins, even when it would have served your immediate needs better to crush your opponent.

For motivation, the main thing is to discover your big why. This is the one thing that has propelled leaders in business, politics, sports, and academics to the pinnacle of their respective fields. Anyone who wants to become a good leader must first search within themselves for their purpose and only do things that help them get there. And at the workplace, everything you do ought to be in service to the vision that you set. In fact, you should make the big picture a reference point when making your to-do list for greater motivation.

We also touched on stress and anxiety management among leaders. Stress management is an area most managers struggle at, but with simple NLP techniques, we discussed how you can ensure that your mind and body are always relaxed and primed for action. With anxiety, it is better to try to make use of it rather than straight out avoiding (or trying to). The anxious mind has been found to be highly effective by studies as recent as 2017, and our "Allow, Befriend, and Channel" (ABC) strategy ought to help you harness anxiety to bring flow to your work and increase productivity.

If you are to take one thing from this book, let it be vision setting and pursuing. A good vision is key to solving every problem that a junior manager like you faces. As a bonus, let the second lesson be using NLP to pursue the excellence you desire.

And there you go, the complete guide to leadership using NLP as promised. A solution for every communication, decision making, vision setting, stress coping, and adopting concern you will ever have as you settle into your new office. I hope you have as enjoyable and transformation a journey reading this book as I had written it. All the best!

Hello,

To fully master new NLP techniques, it´s best if you repeat them several times.

For your convenience we have assembled a PDF document with 34 most important NLP Techniques for you as a busy entrepreneur.

You can print these PDF or parts of these PDF as much as you want. You can place the NLP Technique where it´s the most convenient for you. This can be your bathroom mirror, the fridge in your kitchen or the monitor at your business. Whatever works for you.

If you want to be a productive entrepreneur:

Go to: https://businessleadershipplatform.com/nlp-for-leadership

or

Get the PDF with the 34 NLP techniques for Leadership

Print (parts of the) PDF

Start applying the NLP Techniques to **10x your business**

Now you´re ready to dive into the book.

Jonatan Slane

Business Leadership Platform

www.businessleadershipplatform.com

References

Aventis (2018). Effective presentation skills: Engage your audience with NLP Strategies. *Aventis Learning Group.* Retrieved from https://aventislearning.com/effective-presentation-skills-engage-your-audience-with-nlp-strategies/ on 24th August 2019

Bandler, R. (2018). Time management and task-switching by Dr. Richard Bandler. *NLP Life.* Retrieved from https://www.nlplifetraining.com/content/time-management-and-task-switching-dr-richard-bandler on 22nd August 2019

Basu, R. (2009). NLP techniques, decision making with timeline. *The NLP Company.* Retrieved from http://www.thenlpcompany.com/therapy/nlp-techniques-decision-making-with-time-line/ on 22nd August 2019

Basu, R. (2016). Feel good techniques to increase productivity. *The NLP Company.* Retrieved from http://www.thenlpcompany.com/job-hunting/feel-good-techniques-increase-productivity/ on 22nd August 2019

Beale, M. (2019). What is NLP | Confirmation bias. *NLP Techniques.* Retrieved from https://www.nlp-techniques.org/what-is-nlp/confirmation-bias/ on 21st August 2019

Chang, C. (2014). NLP Singapore – Greatest entrepreneurs of all times & what we can learn from them (part 2 of 3). *N.L.P. Academy.* Retrieved from http://www.nlpinsingapore.com/tag/richard-branson on 19th August 2019

Excellence Academy. (2018). How to find your higher purpose using NLP. *Excellence Academy.* Retrieved from https://excellenceacademy.com.au/how-to-find-your-higher-purpose-using-nlp/ on 20th August 2019

Excellence Assured. (2017). Goal setting with your timeline in mind. *Excellency Assured.* Retrieved from https://excellenceassured.com/2402/goal-setting-with-your-timeline-in-mind on 20th August 2019

Excellence Assured (n.d). NLP language technique for negotiation. *Excellence Assured.* Retrieved from https://excellenceassured.com/1906/nlp-language-technique-for-negotiation on 25th August 2019

Farrell, W. (2016). The 4 D's of time management. *Coaching with NLP*. Retrieved from https://www.coachingwithnlp.co/4-ds-of-time-management/ on 22nd August 2019

Frossell, S. (2007). Communicating more effectively with NLP. *Sarah Frossell LLP*. Retrieved from http://www.sarahfrossell.com/article4.htm on 24th August 2019

Gallo, C. (2012). 11 presentation lessons you can still learn from Steve Jobs. *Forbes*. Retrieved from https://www.forbes.com/sites/carminegallo/2012/10/04/11-presentation-lessons-you-can-still-learn-from-steve-jobs/#5b75bfd8dde3 on 24th August 2019

Harrison, C. (2012). NLP business benefits – What are the benefits of NLP in a business or sales environment? *Planet NLP*. Retrieved from http://www.planetnlp.com/nlp_business_benefits.html on 19th August 2019

Harrison, C. (2013) NLP techniques. *Planet NLP*. Retrieved from http://www.planetnlp.com/nlp_techniques.html on 20th August 2019

Illiopoulos, A. (2018). 5 critical mental models to add to your cognitive repertoire. *Medium*. Retrieved from https://medium.com/personal-growth/mental-models-898f70438075 on 21st August 2019

Illumine (2012). NLP and effective communication. *Illumine Training*. Retrieved from https://www.illumine.co.uk/2012/02/nlp-and-effective-communication/ on 23rd August 2019

James, T. (2019). What is NLP? A model of communication and personality. *The Tad James Company*. Retrieved from https://www.nlpcoaching.com/what-is-nlp-a-model-of-communication-and-personality/ on 24th August 2019

Marquis, D. (2019). What is NLP? These 4 techniques could change how you think. *Happiness*. Retrieved from https://www.happiness.com/en/magazine/personal-growth/nlp-happiness-techniques/ on 21st August 2019

Matthew, B. J. (2019). What is NLP? *The Empowerment Partnership*. Retrieved from http://www.nlp.com/what-is-nlp/ on 19th August 2019

NLP Notes (2019). Internal Maps of The World. *NLP Notes.* Retrieved from http://nlpnotes.com/internal-maps-of-the-world/ on 19th August 2019

Sanders, R. (2016). 3 NLP techniques to reduce anxiety right now. *Robert Sanders Coaching.* Retrieved from http://www.robertsanders.me.uk/3-nlp-techniques-to-reduce-anxiety-right-now/ on 26th August 2019

Schneider, N. (2017). 5 ways to improve your productivity. *Global NLP Training.* Retrieved from https://www.globalnlptraining.com/blog/5-ways-improve-productivity/ on 22nd August 2019

Schneider, N. (2017). NLP motivation strategy. *Global NLP.* Retrieved from https://www.globalnlptraining.com/blog/nlp-motivation-strategy/ on 28th August 2019

Shervington, M. (2018). How to use NLP to skyrocket your negotiation skills. *The Coaching Room.* Retrieved from https://www.thecoachingroom.com.au/blog/ho

w-to-use-nlp-to-skyrocket-your-negotiation-skills 25th August 2019

Sussman, A. (2016). Stress reduction using NLP: 3 part exercise. *Anxiety Control Center*. Retrieved from https://anxietycontrolcenter.com/stress-reduction-using-nlp-part-1/ on 26th August 2019

The Coaching Room. (n.d.). 15 ways to boost your motivation with NLP. *The Coaching Room*. Retrieved from https://www.thecoachingroom.com.au/hubfs/15_Tips/15_Tips_to_Boost_Motivation.pdf on 28th August 2019

The Maven Circle (2016). A basic guide to NLP and managing anxiety. *The Maven Circle*. Retrieved from https://www.themavencircle.com/managing-anxiety-with-nlp/ on 26th August 2019

Young, M. (2015). 3 powerful techniques to create rapport – fast! *The Coaching Room*. Retrieved from https://www.thecoachingroom.com.au/blog/3-powerful-nlp-techniques-to-create-rapport-fast on 23rd August 20

Printed in Great Britain
by Amazon